NAPA LANDMARKS, INC.
P.O. Box 702, Napa, Ca. 94558

P9-DWY-542

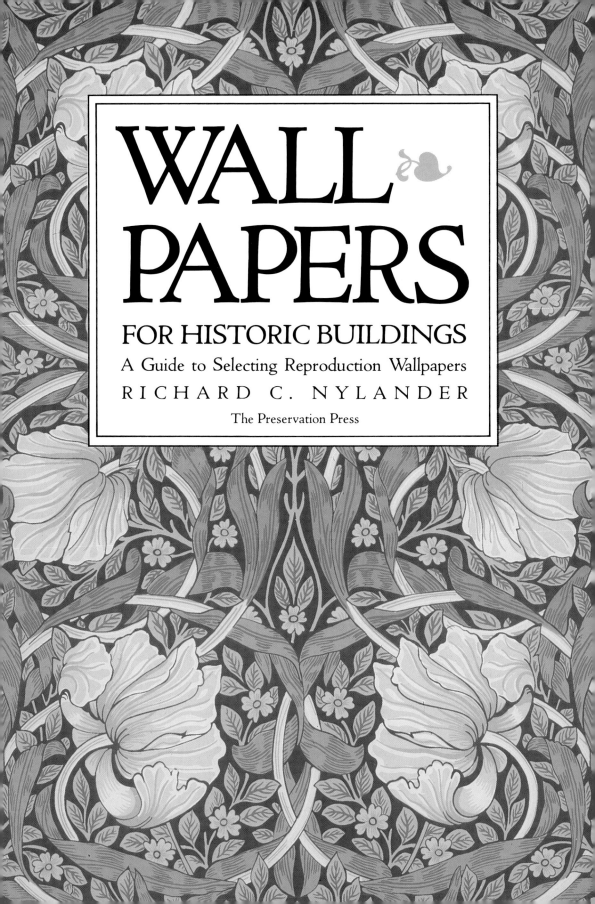

WALL
PAPERS

FOR HISTORIC BUILDINGS

A Guide to Selecting Reproduction Wallpapers

RICHARD C. NYLANDER

The Preservation Press

The Preservation Press
National Trust for Historic Preservation
1785 Massachusetts Avenue, N.W.
Washington, D.C. 20036

The National Trust for Historic Preservation is the only private, non-profit national organization chartered by Congress to encourage public participation in the preservation of sites, buildings and objects significant in American history and culture. Support is provided by membership dues, endowment funds, contributions and grants from federal agencies, including the U.S. Department of the Interior, under provisions of the National Historic Preservation Act of 1966. For information about membership, write to the Trust at the above address.

Printed in the United States of America
92 91 90 89 88   8 7 6 5 4

Library of Congress Cataloging in Publication Data

Nylander, Richard C.
    Wallpapers for historic buildings.

    Bibliography: p.
    1. Wallpaper — Reproduction — Catalogs.   I. Title.
NK3399.N94 1983   747.3   83-10922
ISBN 0-89133-110-7

Richard C. Nylander is curator of collections, Society for the Preservation of New England Antiquities.

The Preservation Press gratefully acknowledges the assistance of Scalamandré in the production of the cover.

Cover: PIMPERNEL, 1876. Designed by William Morris. Scalamandré. (See page 119.)

Endleaves: SAVANNAH TULIP, c. 1900. Scalamandré. (See page 94.)

Pages 6–7: THE MONUMENTS OF PARIS, 1814. The Twigs. (See page 65.)

Pages 20–21: EXETER FAN, 1800–20. Brunschwig and Fils. (See page 35.)

CONTENTS

9 Wallpapers for Historic Buildings   INTRODUCTION

23 1700 to 1780: The English Influence   CATALOG OF
24 ❧ Wallpapers   REPRODUCTION
30 ❧ Nonrepeating Chinese Designs   WALLPAPERS

33 1780 to 1840: Imports and American Patterns
35 ❧ Wallpapers
59 ❧ Borders
63 ❧ Plain Papers
63 ❧ Scenic Papers

67 1840 to 1870: Revival Styles and Machine Printing
69 ❧ Wallpapers
79 ❧ Borders

81 1870 to 1910: Stylized Designs for the Late Victorian Era
82 ❧ Wallpapers
101 ❧ Borders, Dados and Panels
106 ❧ Ceiling Papers
111 ❧ Oatmeal Papers
111 ❧ Embossed Papers
112 ❧ Anaglypta
115 ❧ Scenic Papers
115 ❧ William Morris–Style Papers

121 Manufacturers   APPENDIX
123 Glossary
124 Selected Bibliography
126 Sources of Information
127 Acknowledgments

INTRODUCTION

WALLPAPERS FOR HISTORIC BUILDINGS

Wallpapers have always been a popular means of enhancing interior spaces in both domestic and public buildings, for they fill otherwise blank walls with a wide variety of design and color. Reproduction wallpaper can be an important element in the decoration of historic buildings.

Like carpets and textiles, wallpaper was chosen to make a room fashionable, to complement its architecture and to provide a unifying background for its furnishings. Once applied to the walls, however, wallpaper became a part of the structure. Unlike carpets and textiles, it could not be moved and incorporated into another decorative scheme. When wallpaper became worn or unfashionable, it no longer fulfilled its purpose and was either covered or removed. Thus, fewer samples of historic wallpaper survive than do examples of other decorative interior elements.

Wallpaper design and its use in American buildings have not been explored as extensively as other decorative arts. One reason is that few major collections of historic wallpaper samples exist. Moreover, the written records most often relied on when researching a historic house — estate inventories and probate deeds, for example—seldom document the use of wallpaper. Consequently, the importance of wallpaper in the decoration of a room has never been considered as seriously as other aspects of the restoration process.

In the introduction to *Wallpaper in America*, a recent book on the subject, Catherine Lynn quotes the title of a pamphlet written in 1880 — "What Shall We Do with Our Walls?" The question is a valid one and one that should be considered by every property owner and restoration committee dedicated to restoring a historic building accurately. A quick survey, however, reveals that little attention has been paid to this question. During the past three decades the most popular solution has been to paint the walls white. This approach has conveyed the false impression that before the Victorian period rooms were stark, the only color coming from elaborate draperies at the windows and oriental rugs on the floors. Lynn notes that in the late 19th century — the peak period of wallpaper production and use — white walls were considered "relics of barbarism,

Hanging a reproduction architecture paper, 1898, South Berwick, Maine.

and almost a thing of the past." Today, in contrast, these same white walls have become almost a symbol of traditional historic decoration.

Whitewash, an easy and effective treatment for walls, was used extensively in the 18th century. Wallpaper, when first produced, was a luxury. Anyone who could afford expensive furniture and textiles would have also wanted to complement this display of wealth and taste by hanging paper on the walls of the house. As wallpaper became increasingly available and affordable, it became the typical wall treatment. In 1850 Andrew Jackson Downing wrote in his popular and useful book *The Architecture of Country Houses*: "We confess a strong partiality for the use of paper-hangings for covering the walls of cottages." He goes on to say that one advantage is "in the enhanced architectural effect which may be given to a plain room, by covering the walls with a paper of suitable style."

The use of reproduction wallpaper and the choice of a particular pattern depend on the purpose of the restoration, rehabilitation or redecoration of the historic building. The information included here is intended to serve as a guide for curators and committees of museum houses whose aim is to convey an accurate impression of a building's former appearance or create an accurate period interpretation, for homeowners who are seeking wallpapers that are appropriate to the architectural style of a historic house or that provide a sympathetic background for collection of antiques, and for people who wish to introduce a period look to a rehabilitation or adaptive use project.

This book presents reproductions of historic wallpapers that are currently available. The original documents from which the designs are copied date from 1700 to 1910, and the information is organized according to historical period. A short essay introducing popular patterns and technology precedes each section. The works cited in the bibliography should be consulted for their illustrations and detailed information on the history of wallpaper design and production.

The author confesses a strong partiality towards the appropriate use of reproduction wallpaper in restoration and rehabilitation projects, and it is hoped that the papers included here will help restorers of historic buildings paper the walls in a style suitable to the purpose of the restoration.

HISTORY OF REPRODUCTION WALLPAPERS

The interest in old wallpaper patterns seems to have begun in the late 19th century. One impetus was the centennial celebration, which caused Americans to look at their own past. Local groups became concerned about the fate of buildings considered historically important to their communities, and architects began to study early American buildings for design inspiration. Interest in the American past was also reflected in interior decoration; imitating the historic styles of European decoration was no longer the only option. The fashionable American interior acquired a certain charm and aura of stability with the inclusion of an heirloom chair found in grandmother's attic or a piece of old china

Reproduction "Lady Pepperrell House" installed in the room in which the document paper, c. 1760, was found. Lady Pepperrell House, Kittery Point, Maine.

purchased during an afternoon outing of "antiquing."

In a chatty book entitled *Old Time Wall Papers,* published in 1905, Kate Sanborn indicates that wallpaper manufacturers had responded to a demand for papers appropriate for Colonial Revival houses and that wallpapers reproducing old designs were readily available. Indeed, before 1900, several historical societies and even a few private owners of old houses had commissioned custom reproductions of early papers they had found on the walls of the buildings they were restoring. (It is interesting to note that Sanborn considered wallpaper reproductions an "expensive matter," the price per roll in 1905 being $6 to $10.)

During the first quarter of the 20th century, reproduction wallpapers and papers incorporating earlier design motifs became standard offerings of many wallpaper manufacturers. Firms such as Thomas Strahan Company in Chelsea, Mass., and M.H. Birge Company in Buffalo, N.Y., specialized in such papers. The documents from which the designs were taken dated almost exclusively before 1850, and from the 1920s to the 1940s these so-called colonial papers adorned the walls of a vast number of both privately and publicly owned historic houses.

The extensive use of reproduction papers in older houses coincided with a general use of wallpaper in most American homes in the early 20th century. In the mid-20th century, the preference for unadorned, white walls in modern interiors influenced the tastes of committee members in charge of the decoration of museum houses. When the wall surfaces needed to be renewed, the reproduction wallpapers that had been hung only a generation earlier were taken down and the walls painted white. Today, the pendulum is swinging back. Modern designers and homeowners are incorporating wallpaper into their decorative schemes. Museum curators are no longer content to display just a small sample of antique wallpaper in a room whose walls were once covered with it; they consider the paper an integral part of the room's historic decoration and are having it reproduced in an effort to present as accurate an impression of the past as possible.

RESEARCH

Paint and wallpaper are the two elements of any previous decorative scheme that are most likely to remain in a building as evidence of the tastes of the original and subsequent occupants. The probability that wallpaper was used as a decorative finish in a building should be considered from the outset of a restoration project, not at the end. Time should be taken to examine the structure for all evidence it may yield. Often, potentially helpful wallpaper evidence is overlooked in the rush to begin structural rehabilitation of a building. Photographs should be taken before any investigation is begun and as work proceeds. Each wallpaper remaining on the walls should be examined to determine its age; it is not inconceivable that one may be an early paper or perhaps the original paper. No wallpaper should be removed until a historical period for the restoration or redecoration has been established. If the decision is made to retain an early paper, a paper conservator should be consulted about whether cleaning and readhesion are necessary.

A room whose walls have been stripped to the bare plaster is not necessarily devoid of wallpaper evidence. Plaster that has never been painted is an indication that the walls had a decorative covering from the outset—most likely a wallpaper.

Check all surfaces of the room, including the ceiling, for wallpaper evidence. Later architectural changes may obscure an early wallpaper. Often a room was divided. Occasionally a new wall was built in front of an old one. Other elements, such as door and window casings, baseboards and mantels, were often replaced in an effort to "modernize" a room. Cupboards may have been built in, or a Victorian picture molding may have been applied just below the ceiling. Even electrical switchplates may conceal a small fragment of early wallpaper. Often, large pieces of furniture, such as bookcases or mirrors secured to the walls, were not moved when a room was repapered.

When a wallpaper sample is located, it should be photographed for recording purposes in both color and black and white, as color photographs have a tendency to fade. The sample's location should be noted on a sketch of the wall plan.

The thickness of a paper sample removed from the walls can be deceiving. Often, it contains more than one layer. Before the invention of the wallpaper steamer, removing the existing layer of paper when a new paper was applied was not common practice; only loose or damaged portions were removed so the new paper would lie flat. The layers of a wallpaper "sandwich" can be separated by careful steaming or soaking. One sandwich separated by the author contained 27 layers of paper, recording the decoration of the room from which it was removed from about 1780 until a matchboard dado was installed in the 1930s.

When wallpaper is found, a record should be kept for each sample, noting the room from which it was removed and, if part of a sandwich, its place in the sequence of layers. Small fragments should not be considered worthless. They are an important part of the sequence and may be identified fully if a larger sample of the pattern exists in another wallpaper collection.

If no wallpaper samples are found in the structure itself, information may be obtained from other sources. For example, objects associated with former occupants should be studied. Leftover wallpaper was used for a variety of purposes, such as sealing the backs of framed pictures, covering homemade diaries and account books and making small boxes. Wallpapers found in trunks or on band boxes should be carefully researched, however. Some of the small-figured designs used for trunk linings were manufactured specifically for that purpose and were not used to paper rooms. The same is true for many of the large, continuous designs found on hat boxes. Interior photographs taken in the late 19th or early 20th centuries may record the design of a wallpaper that has since been removed. Many successful reproduction wallpaper patterns have been reconstructed from early photographs.

All wallpaper evidence should be combined and coordinated with a thorough search of the documents relating to the building and its occupants. Although the initial idea may be to restore a building to its original appearance, complete information about all the components of its interior finishes and furnishings may not exist. Documentation on the wallpaper, textiles and furniture used at a later date may be more extensive. A broad research project will place the building in an architectural context within the community as well as establish the socioeconomic level of its various occupants. Research may reveal additional references to wallpaper; more important, it can help establish a historical period for the restoration.

The wallpaper samples, in effect, evince the tastes of the former occupants. If the date of a sample coincides with the historical period established for the restoration, its design can probably be duplicated in a custom-made reproduction. However, if the expense is too great, the sample can be used as a guide in choosing a similar pattern that is available as a commercial reproduction.

If no samples of wallpaper are found in a historic building, choosing an appropriate reproduction is more difficult. Research into secondary sources is necessary to answer general questions about wallpaper: What patterns were available? What styles were fashionable? Where was wallpaper purchased? In what rooms was it most often used? These questions, asked within the framework of the documentary research on the building itself and the research into the historical period of the restoration, can help determine the type of wallpaper pattern to select.

In 1787, after looking at the wallpapers available for his new house, a Boston merchant wrote, "There are so great a variety of Fashions, I am totally at a loss as to what kind to get." Today, an owner of a historic building may have the same experience when trying to choose a pattern from the variety of reproductions available. The Boston merchant concluded that a person's choice of wallpaper "principally depends on fancy." Like today's homeowner, he was trying to choose a paper that was not only fashionable but also appealing to him. Those responsible for a museum restoration, however, do not have the same latitude in their selection. The choice of a reproduction wallpaper should not be subject to the 20th-century restorer's taste. Reproduction wallpaper should be chosen within the bounds of the prevailing taste of the restoration period.

WHAT TO LOOK FOR IN A REPRODUCTION

The term "documentary design" is often loosely interpreted. Many wallpaper sample books labeled "The Colonial Collection" include designs that have no relationship to the wallpapers used during the 18th century. Rather, these designs are the traditional, usually small-figured patterns that have become associated with older houses. Many interpretive designs are created by reworking motifs from historic documents—not necessarily wallpapers — into new patterns.

Even when a wallpaper is part of a collection licensed by a museum or preservation organization, the source of the design may be a printed or woven fabric, a book endpaper or a motif from a sampler, a quilt or a ceramic plate. These are attractive designs created to appeal to current popular taste and to complement a manufacturer's collection or line. However evocative of the past, such designs have nothing to do with historic wallpaper patterns and are not recommended for use in historic buildings being accurately restored. This book lists only those documentary designs derived from wallpapers.

The reproduction wallpapers available today fall into two categories: (1) accurate reproductions and (2) adaptations. An accurate reproduction follows exactly the design, scale (including width and repeat) and color of the original document. An adaptation achieves the overall look and spirit of the original paper, but certain changes have been made by the manufacturer. The design and scale may have been altered; a motif may have been reworked or a new one introduced; the colors may have been printed weaker or stronger than the original, or one new color may have been added.

The question to consider with adaptations is how far the design of the document can be reworked before it becomes a new pattern. An adaptation should not be chosen if the scale has been substantially reduced or enlarged, if a major motif has not been included or an incongruous one introduced or if it includes a color that had not been invented when the original paper was produced. Again, always check a paper labeled as an adaptation; its source may not have been a wallpaper.

Even an accurate reproduction cannot exactly duplicate the original wallpaper. The production methods and materials used in printing a reproduction wallpaper differ substantially from those used to create the historic paper. Although some reproduction papers are printed with rollers, the majority are produced with silk screens.

Both screen- and roller-printed papers use commercially available ground papers on which the design is printed. Modern ground papers do not have the texture of 18th-century handmade paper, nor are they as thin as the cheap machine-made paper on which many late Victorian designs were printed.

Modern ground papers come in standard widths. These widths are wider than those of historic papers, which usually ranged from 18 to 23 inches, depending on the date and country of origin. All-over patterns with small horizontal repeats can easily be accommodated on modern widths. Although more horizontal repeats can fit on today's wider paper, the scale remains the same. Occasionally, the scale of the document design has to be adjusted slightly to fill the modern width. (Such adjustment is often necessary for papers that are pretrimmed.) The horizontal repeat of a large design often cannot be adjusted to fill a modern width. The original width, therefore, is copied, leaving a wider than usual margin on each side. Although these margins may appear to be a waste of paper, the manufacturer compensates for it by increasing the length of the roll, so that the area the paper covers meets the standard of approximately 30 square feet per roll.

The silk-screen method of printing best imitates the look of a block-printed paper. The definition of line and the thickness of pigment of the original are lost when an 18th-century design is printed with a roller, and the overall pattern appears weak. Conversely, a late Victorian roller-printed paper that is reproduced today by the silk-screen process often looks more substantial than the original. The running together of thin colors, which occurred in the rapid roller-printing process of the original, can best be duplicated by machine.

The visual differences created by this change in technology are most apparent when comparing a sample of the historic paper with a sample of the reproduction. However, the differences become minimal when the reproduction paper is installed on the walls of a room.

The changes brought about by modern printing methods and materials are compromises that are generally accepted in restorations today. In essence, then, an acceptable reproduction wallpaper is one in which the design and coloring most closely resemble that of the original.

Manufacturers approach reproduction papers from different points of view. Some reproduce the exact appearance of a historic sample, including faded colors and missing design elements. They may also reproduce a printing flaw found on the original document. Other manufacturers compensate for loss of color or design defects by making the reproduction resemble the appearance of the original when it was new. Although this book includes reproduction papers of both types, current restoration practice favors the latter approach.

CUSTOM-MADE REPRODUCTION WALLPAPERS

Today's manufacturers do not produce reproduction wallpapers exclusively for use in historic buildings. They also sell to a contemporary market and, therefore, must consider current tastes when choosing patterns from historic documents. No manufacturer should be expected to include reproductions of every popular style from each historical period. Often a style most popular in a given period will simply not be appealing today and, thus, will not be found on the market.

Given the variety of patterns of historic wallpaper, the odds that a paper found in a particular historic building has already been reproduced are slim. Custom work may be the only means of obtaining an exact copy of a paper needed for an accurate restoration project. If the wallpaper samples found in a building are appropriate to the historical period of the restoration and if a complete design exists, having the paper custom reproduced may be preferable to choosing a pattern from those commercially available. The goal of custom work is as accurate a reproduction as possible in terms of design, color, scale and simulation of the original printing technique. Neither the client nor the manufacturer should "improve" the design; unclear lines and faded colors should not be used to give the paper an "antique" look.

Most wallpaper firms will consider custom work, but it is an expensive and time-consuming procedure. The client is responsible for all costs incurred, including the artwork, the cost of each silk screen, the set-up and printing expenses. The client is also responsible for approving both the artwork before the screens are cut and the strike-offs for final color. Custom work may require the client to order a minimum number of rolls; it is always wise to order enough to paper a room twice in case damage occurs.

It is popularly believed that a wallpaper manufacturer will happily reproduce any sample of wallpaper found in a historic building, include the reproduction in a commercial line and donate enough paper to paper one room of the building. In reality, the manufacturer rarely does any of these things. A firm may wish to add the reproduction to its line if the design is considered appealing by today's standards. In this case, a royalty arrangement should be negotiated and confirmed by a written contract. The manufacturers may also wish to produce the design in other color combinations, called colorways. If a client approves such a proposal, he or she should obtain royalties on all colorways produced.

PERIOD INSTALLATION

Once a reproduction wallpaper has been chosen, some attention should be paid to its installation. While the basic methods of applying paper to walls

have not changed, certain period practices should be noted.

Although paste has always been the most common means of attaching paper to walls, some early wallpapers were held in place with small tacks. Lining paper was not commonly used during the 18th and 19th centuries.

Most wallpapers today, including many of the reproduction papers, are pretrimmed. Papers produced in the 18th and 19th centuries had an unprinted margin, or selvage, on each side. Usually only one selvage was cut off, and the seams were overlapped when the paper was hung. Today, the preferred method of hanging an untrimmed paper is to cut off both margins and butt the edges.

Board or sheathed walls were frequently papered instead of painted. Before paper was applied, thin strips of cloth were pasted over the joints of the boards so the paper would lie flat and not split or be punctured. Plaster dados under a chair rail were often papered rather than painted the color of the woodwork. Corner posts found in early buildings were not usually papered until the late 19th century.

In the 18th and early 19th centuries, fireboards used to cover the fireplace opening during the summer months were often papered. Some papers were designed with this specific purpose in mind, although many fireboards were covered with the same paper and border used in the rest of the room.

The most important consideration when installing reproduction

Custom-made wallpaper and borders, reproducing the original English papers installed in 1796. Borders outline the woodwork, following evidence found in the room. Harrison Gray Otis House, Boston, Mass.

17

Photograph, taken in 1911, of an American wallpaper installed incorrectly around 1800. Short House, Newbury, Mass.

wallpaper — particularly when attempting an accurate restoration — is the use of a border. Borders were an important part of wallpaper design and were used to some degree in every historical period discussed. Often borders were an integral part of the overall pattern; others were designed to complement the design of the sidewall. But some found in historic buildings bear no relationship to the paper with which they were used.

The extent to which borders were used in a room varies. In some cases they surrounded all the architectural elements; in other cases they were used only at the ceiling level (or just below the cornice) or at both the ceiling level and above the chair rail or baseboard. Often a border at the ceiling level was wider than the one used elsewhere in the room; also, it may have been of a completely different design. The borders in different rooms of a building may have been treated differently.

Where borders were used in a room also varied during different historical periods. During the 18th century borders were commonly used to outline the architecture of a room; each wall was treated as a separate unit, so that two widths of borders appeared in each corner. With the exception of bordering the corners, this practice continued into the early 19th century. The use of borders only around the ceiling and chair rail was also fashionable. In the mid-19th century borders were sometimes used to divide a room into a series of panels. Late 19th-century paper-hangers used borders to divide the wall into three horizontal units. These general principles should be kept in mind while investigating the structure and searching for evidence that will indicate how the room was bordered.

Locating an old photograph that illustrates how the wallpaper was installed in a room can be a great help in researching an accurate restoration; it can also create a dilemma. The photograph of the parlor of the Short House, Newbury, Mass. (page 18), shows the best parlor of an early 18th-century house as it looked in 1911. Samples of the paper survive and date between 1800 and 1810. However, whoever hung the paper obviously did not understand the pattern. Other photographs of the room show the cornice border applied vertically in the corners and alongside the windows and doors. It was also used to outline a dado created by hanging a floral pattern horizontally. Should this evidence be precisely duplicated in hanging the reproduction wallpaper, or should the period mistake be corrected? The final decision depends on the purpose of the restoration or rehabilitation. In some cases, such mistakes have been corrected.

HOW TO USE THE CATALOG

The following catalog of reproduction wallpapers is arranged by historical period. Borders, dados and panels have been separated from sidewall papers and are listed at the end of each section. The following types of wallpapers are listed separately for the appropriate historical period: nonrepeating patterns and plain ground papers; scenic papers; ceiling papers; embossed papers; and papers designed by or in the style of William Morris.

Individual catalog entries give the following information when it is available:

Manufacturer's catalog name for the wallpaper pattern
Country, date and method of manufacture of the original
Source of a published photograph of the document wallpaper (see bibliography for complete titles)
Width, repeat and roll content (yards per single roll ["s/r"]) of reproduction wallpaper
Changes made by the manufacturer in the reproduction
Organization or museum for which the wallpaper was reproduced
Information about the document and its location
Manufacturer's catalog number for the reproduction wallpaper
Manufacturer's name for the document color or description of the document color (an alternate color may occasionally be listed; this is a colorway produced by the manufacturer that, although not necessarily from a document, is a plausible period coloring for the design)
Note: An asterisk after a catalog entry denotes a wallpaper that has a definite period look in terms of design and color but is not listed as a reproduction or adaptation and whose exact source is unknown to the author or manufacturer

Remember that wallpaper is priced by the single roll but sold in double- or triple-roll quantities. Make sure the room being papered is measured accurately and the repeat of the pattern is figured into the calculations to determine the number of rolls needed.

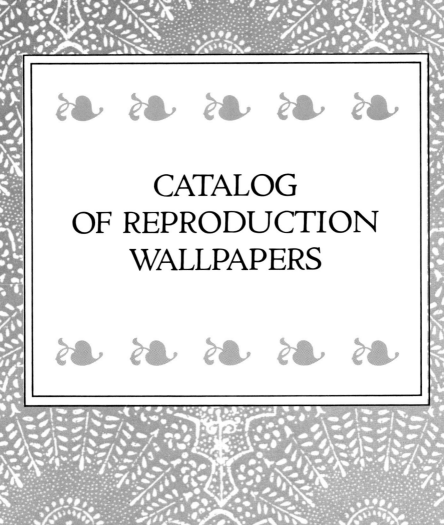

CATALOG
OF REPRODUCTION
WALLPAPERS

1700 TO 1780:
THE ENGLISH INFLUENCE

The earliest reference to wallpaper in America, according to Catherine Lynn, is recorded in the inventory of a Boston stationer in 1700. In the first half of the 18th century, painted paper hangings were found only in houses of wealthy city dwellers. Americans who could afford wallpaper purchased it either from stationers or booksellers who dealt in an entire range of paper goods or from merchants as special orders. The availability and use of wallpaper increased steadily from 1750. Toward the end of the 18th century, wallpaper was also purchased from upholsterers, the equivalent of modern interior designers.

In the 18th century, wallpaper was most commonly printed with wood blocks. Occasionally, stencils and handwork were used. Individual sheets of handmade paper were pasted together to form a roll, because it was not possible to produce the continuous roll of paper we know today. When the roll was made up, it received a ground color, which was applied with large brushes. Finally, the pattern was printed with a series of wood blocks, one for each color and unit of the design.

A roll of paper was called a "piece." This terminology, along with the use of the smaller sheets of paper to form a roll, has led to the misconception that early wallpapers were hung by pasting each separate sheet onto the wall. Although this method of application was sometimes used with the earliest papers, careful examination of a sample of 18th-century paper will reveal no color under the horizontal seam where the sheets are joined. Examination of the design indicates that the size of the repeat (and, therefore, the size of the block used to print it) is rarely the same as the size of the individual piece of paper.

Although the two earliest wallpapers that have been reproduced are "Charles II" and "Cerises," probably neither was used in American houses. "Charles II" (page 22) is a copy of a black-and-white woodblock print made in England between 1690 and 1700. "Cerises" (page 25) reproduces a "domino" paper made around 1750. These early French papers are named after the group of craftsmen called "dominotiers," who specialized in simple one- or two-color prints. "Charles II" and "Cerises" were originally printed on single sheets, not rolls, and were most often used as decorative endpapers for books or as trunk linings.

CHARLES II, 1690–1710. Katzenbach and Warren. Black on white.

Most wallpapers used in American buildings before the Revolution were of English origin. The patterns available in the mid-18th century can be separated into several distinct types. Most expensive were the custom-made hangings, i.e., those made specifically to fit the walls of a new house. Notable examples of this type of paper can be found in the Jeremiah Lee Manison (1768) in Marblehead, Mass., and in the Van Rensselaer Hall (1768) installed in the American Wing of the Metropolitan Museum of Art. Both depict classical ruins copied from prints and are surrounded with large trompe l'oeil frames. They were designed to imitate walls hung with large framed paintings. Wallpapers with repeating patterns simulating walls hung with smaller framed prints, such as "Lady Pepperrell House" (pages 11 and 31), were more readily available.

Architecture papers were a popular 18th-century style of paper that is not reproduced today. A more descriptive name for these large-figured designs was "pillar and arch" papers. Newspaper advertisements recommended them as most appropriate for use in entries, the 18th-century term for staircase halls. In the 1898 photograph depicting a paper-hanger at work (page 8), the paper being hung is a reproduction of an 18th-century architecture paper.

Other large-scale patterns imitated the more expensive silk and wool damasks used to cover the walls of the most elaborate English houses; see, for example, "Peyton Randolph" (page 27). These papers were made to look even more like fabric by means of flocking, a process in which small fragments of chopped wool or silk were spread over the paper, adhering where the design had been printed with a varnish instead of a color. Flocked papers were expensive; evidence of their use has been found primarily in parlors and best chambers.

Because hand-painted papers from China with nonrepeating patterns were expensive, few were found in American buildings. However, the designs were admired, and English manufacturers often incorporated individual motifs into repeating patterns to create wallpapers in the Chinese style.

The greatest variety in patterns was to be found in wallpapers with floral or small-figured designs. Because of their scale and motifs, these types of 18th-century design appeal most to 20th-century tastes and consequently are most often reproduced and adapted for use today.

WALLPAPERS

BRUNSCHWIG AND FILS

&❧ CERISES. French, 1750–60, block print. 26¾" wide, 4¼" repeat, 5 yds. per s/r. Document at Musée des Arts Décoratifs, Paris. No. 12581.06 (brick and blue).

&❧ CHINA FANCY. English, 1750–80, block print. 21½" wide, 43" drop repeat, 6 yds. per s/r. Colors not reproduced exactly. Document at Winterthur Museum. No. 10771.06 (pink and jade on ivory).

&❧ CHINOISERIE. French, 1770–90, block print. 24" wide, 36" repeat, 5 yds. per s/r. Reproduced for Museum of Early Southern Decorative

CERISES, 1750–60.
Brunschwig and Fils.
Brick and blue.

MANDARIN AND
PINE TREE, 1690–1730.
Katzenbach and Warren.
Brown and black on white.

DORCHESTER, 1760–80.
Brunschwig and Fils. Rose
on black.

PEYTON RANDOLPH, 1750–70. Katzenbach and Warren. Blue.

Arts. Document in Brunschwig Archives. No. 610.06 (lacquer red and blue on parchment).

❧ DORCHESTER. English or French, 1760–80, block print. 21″ wide, 22½″ repeat, 6 yds. per s/r. Document at Society for the Preservation of New England Antiquities. No. 11049.06 (rose on black).

COLE AND SON

❧ TEMPLE NEWSAM. English, 1720–40, block print with flock. 21″ wide, 21″ repeat, 11 yds. per s/r. Reproduction not flocked. No. 98801 (green on white). Special order. Custom color can be printed.

KATZENBACH AND WARREN

❧ CHARLES II. English, 1690–1710, block print. Oman and Hamilton, fig. 26, p. 97. 20¼″ wide, 14¼″ repeat, 7 yds. per s/r. Document at Colonial Williamsburg. No. 60-0058-9 (black on white).

❧ LAFAYETTE FLORAL. English, 1770–90, block print. 20½″ wide, 22″ repeat, 7 yds. per s/r. Document at Colonial Williamsburg. Sample at Society for the Preservation of New England Antiquities. No. 60-0051-4 (blue).

❧ MANDARIN AND PINE TREE. English, 1690–1730, block print. 20″ wide, 22″ repeat, 7 yds. per s/r. Document at Colonial Williamsburg. No. 60-0044-8 (brown and black on white).

❧ PEYTON RANDOLPH. English, 1750–70, block print with flocking. 27″ wide, 36″ repeat, 5 yds. per s/r. Reproduction not flocked. Document at Colonial Williamsburg. No. 60-0105-4 (blue). Alternate color: No. 60-0105-5 (red).

LAFAYETTE FLORAL,
1770–90. Katzenbach and
Warren. Blue.

CAPTAIN JOHN
KENDRICK HOUSE,
1760–80. Waterhouse
Wallhangings. Black and
white on ochre.

WAREHAM FLORAL, 1770–80. Waterhouse Wallhangings. Pink ground.

THE TWIGS

🍃 LEOPARD. English, 1760–80, block print. 22″ wide, 21¼″ repeat. Original color not reproduced. Alternate colors: No. A161-22 (green and tan); No. A161-23 (blue and tan).

WATERHOUSE WALLHANGINGS

🍃 CAPTAIN JOHN KENDRICK HOUSE. English, 1760–80, block print. 20″ wide, 22″ repeat, 7 yds. per s/r. Document in Waterhouse Archives. No. 177269 (black and white on ochre). Alternate color: No. 177248 (green on gray).

🍃 EAST INDIA. French, 1760–70, block print. Lynn, color plate 20, p. 64. 20½″ wide, 22″ repeat, 7 yds. per s/r. Colors not reproduced exactly. Document at Cooper-Hewitt Museum. No. 158635 (green and orange on white).

🍃 GENERAL SAMUEL McCLELLAN. English, 1770–80, block print. 21″ wide, 22½″ repeat, 7 yds. per s/r. Document privately owned. No. 155947 (gray ground).

🍃 LADY PEPPERRELL HOUSE. English, 1760–70, block print. 23″ wide, 42″ repeat, 5 yds. per s/r. Document at Society for the Preservation of New England Antiquities. No. 182433 (gray on pink).

🍃 WAREHAM FLORAL. English, 1770–80, block print. 21″ wide, 18½″ repeat, 7 yds. per s/r. Document in Waterhouse Archives. No. 176433 (pink ground).

NONREPEATING CHINESE DESIGNS

Nonrepeating Chinese panels similar in style to those popular in the 18th century are available from the following companies: Louis W. Bowen, A.L. Diament and Company, Gracie, Katzenbach and Warren (Williamsburg Wallpapers) and Albert Van Luit and Company (Winterthur Museum Collection). Some of these panels are hand-painted.

LADY PEPPERRELL
HOUSE, 1760–70.
Waterhouse Wallhangings.
Gray on pink.

1780 TO 1840:
IMPORTS AND AMERICAN PATTERNS

The period from 1780 to 1840 witnessed a succession of changes in taste as well as technical improvements in paper-making and printing techniques. The Industrial Revolution led to the invention of machines that could produce a continuous roll of paper and others that could print with rollers. However, the wallpaper industry seems to have been slow to take advantage of this new technology, for these machines became standard equipment only at the end of this period. Use of machine-made paper became common in the 1830s, but woodblocks continued to be the preferred method of printing wallpaper until a decade later.

Wallpapers used in American buildings were increasingly available from a variety of sources. English papers remained popular, but competition from papers produced in France was growing. American manufacturing, which had been discouraged during the colonial period, was well established by 1790. The patterns produced by this newly founded American industry were inspired by or copied directly from imported papers; they were advertised as being equal in quality and less expensive.

Because of the various sources of supply during this period, determining the origin of a paper found in the course of a restoration is often difficult. From 1714 to 1836 English papers were required by law to have a stamp printed on the reverse indicating that a tax on the paper had been paid. This stamp usually comprises an interlace of the letters *GR* surmounted with a crown. Although the stamp indicates the origin of the paper, it is of little help in dating the sample. American and French papers, on the other hand, were rarely stamped. The earliest papers produced in America were not necessarily cruder than their European counterparts; in fact, the quality of inexpensive English and French papers was sometimes quite poor.

With the exception of the custom-made hangings imitating large framed paintings, the types of designs described in the previous chapter continued to be popular during the 1780s and into the 1790s. The use of plain colored papers with borders surrounding the architectural elements of the room increased. This type of wall treatment became fashionable in the mid-18th century; the preferred colors were blue or green, and the borders usually were made of papier-mâché. Manufacturers in the late

CRISTAUX, 1825–35.
Brunschwig and Fils. Gray.

33

18th century offered a wider choice of colors for the plain papers and a greater variety in the patterns and widths of the borders.

Except when they copied an imported paper, American wallpapers from 1790 to 1820 are usually simple repeating patterns or stripes, often printed in only one or two colors. See, for example, "Exeter Fan" (pages 20–21), "Dorset" (page 45), "Chesterfield" (page 47), "Coyle House" (page 52), "Enoch Frye" (page 52), "General John Walker" (page 55), "Nye Homestead" (page 57) and "Salem Stripe" (page 58). These, no doubt, were the types of patterns referred to in one Boston manufacturer's advertisement as "common papers."

Beginning in the early 19th century, the importation and use of French wallpapers increased markedly. The French manufacturers had perfected the block-printing process, and their designs and colors clearly captivated the American eye. Until about 1870, French wallpapers dominated the market.

Perhaps the most widely known examples of any historic wallpapers are the French landscape or scenic papers. More examples of this style of paper have been preserved in historic buildings and installed in period room settings in art museums than any other type of historic paper. Antique scenic papers can still be purchased, as well as silk-screen reproductions and reprints from the original blocks. The attention given to scenic papers has often overshadowed other styles of wallpaper that were popular at the same time and used more extensively.

Late 18th-century and early 19th-century French papers excelled in the realistic rendering of both color and shading of flowers, drapery, lace, ribbon, marble, architectural elements and even statuary. See "Ashlar" (page 36), "Bagatelle" (page 38), "Debussy" (page 39), "Fox and Rooster" (page 39), "Birds of Paradise" (page 47), "Bosphore Border" (page 61) and "Charleston Frieze" (page 62). The goal of some designs seems to have been total deception. Many of the classically inspired designs were perfect complements to the new style of Federal architecture. "Maytime" (page 39) and "Louise" (page 56) are reproductions of a French style of paper that was extremely popular from about 1810 until the late 1820s. The basic formula consists of large and small motifs printed alternately on a small-figured background between stripes. An almost endless variety of motifs was plugged into this formula. Today, often only the stripes and small-figured grounds are copied from this style of wallpaper, as these elements appeal most to modern taste. Because the principal motifs are omitted, these adaptations are unsuccessful.

Odile Nouvel's *Wallpapers of France, 1800–1850* presents an impressive survey of the variety of designs found in French papers of the first half of the 19th century. Not all the styles illustrated actually found their way to the United States, but those that did were imitated widely by American manufacturers. Patterns composed of floral motifs, geometric designs and medallions were popular in the 1820s and 1830s. Many French papers of the 1830s are characterized by shaded or blended backgrounds. This process, developed by the Zuber factory, was called "irisée." These papers were referred to as "rainbow papers" in this country and are examples of a type of design that in its own day was popular but that is rarely reproduced today.

BRUNSCHWIG AND FILS   WALLPAPERS

❧ ANANAS. French, 1780–1800, block print. 24¼" wide, 24" repeat, 6 yds. per s/r. Adaptation. Document in Brunschwig Archives (McClelland Collection). No. 11606.06 (persimmon on cream).

❧ ASHLAR. American, 1800–10, block print. 19" wide, 17" repeat, 6 yds. per s/r. Reproduced for Boscobel, Garrison-on-Hudson, N.Y. Document at Society for the Preservation of New England Antiquities. No. 11348.06 (tan).

❧ BAGATELLE. French, 1790–1810, block print. Lynn, color plates 4 and 5, pp. 36, 37. 21" wide, 21" repeat, 7 yds. per s/r. Document at Cooper-Hewitt Museum. No. 12508.06 (brown).

❧ BOSQUET. French, 1798–99, block print. Greysmith, fig. 59, p. 86. 21¼" wide, 20¼" repeat, 6 yds. per s/r. Document at Musée des Arts Décoratifs, Paris. No. 12642.06 (blue).

❧ CRISTAUX. French, 1825–35, block print. Nouvel, fig. 170, p. 61. 18½" wide, 9¼" repeat, 7 yds. per s/r. Document at Musée des Arts Décoratifs, Paris. No. 12599.06 (gray).

❧ DEBUSSY. French, 1825–35, block print. Nouvel, fig. 201, p. 66. 24" wide, 18¼" repeat, 5 yds. per s/r. Document in Brunschwig Archives. No. 11579.06 (pearl gray).

❧ EXETER FAN. American, 1800–20, block print. 28¼" wide, 9½" repeat, 5 yds. per s/r. Document in Brunschwig Archives. No. 11218.06 (beige).

❧ FOX AND ROOSTER. French, 1780–1800, block print. 24" wide, 21" repeat, 6 yds. per s/r. Reproduced for Museum of Early Southern Decorative Arts. Document in Brunschwig Archives. No. 640.06 (rose and blue on clay beige).

❧ FRAMBOISE. French, 1795–1800, block print. 27" wide, 16½" repeat, 5 yds. per s/r. Document at Musée des Arts Décoratifs, Paris. No. 12602.06 (taupe on blue).

❧ GALLIER DIAMOND. French or English, 1800–20, block print. 28" wide, 13⅜" repeat, 5 yds. per s/r. Document in Brunschwig Archives. No. 10410.06 (brown and green on beige).

❧ GEOMETRIQUE. French, 1825–35, block print. 27" wide, 4⅝" repeat, 5 yds. per s/r. Document at Musée des Arts Décoratifs, Paris. No. 12569.06 (gray).

❧ IMLAY. American, 1790–1800, block print. McClelland, p. 258. 20½" wide, 21½" repeat, 5 yds. per s/r. Document at Winterthur Museum. No. 10862.06 (orange and blue on blue).

❧ LOCKLIN PLANTATION. Probably English, 1780–1810, block print. 28¼" wide, 30" repeat, 5 yds. per s/r. Pattern slightly enlarged.

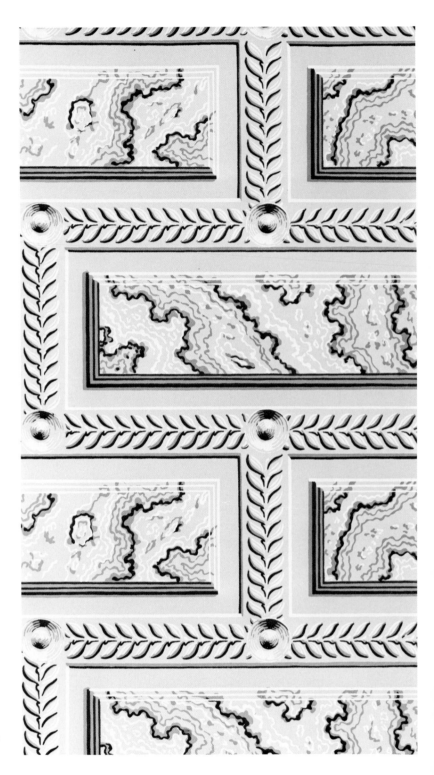

ASHLAR, 1800–10. Brunschwig and Fils. Tan.

GALLIER DIAMOND,
1800–20. Brunschwig and
Fils. Brown and green on
beige.

BAGATELLE, 1790–1810.
Brunschwig and Fils.
Brown.

top left
MAYTIME, 1810–25.
Brunschwig and Fils. Gray
and orange on blue.

top right
DEBUSSY, 1825–35.
Brunschwig and Fils. Pearl
gray.

left
FOX AND ROOSTER,
1780–1800. Brunschwig
and Fils. Rose and blue on
clay beige.

Reproduced for Liberty Hall, Kenansville, N.C. Document in Brunschwig Archives. No. 800.06 (lacquer and blue on beige).

&. MAINTENON. French, 1780–1800, block print. 21″ wide, 25¼″ repeat, 7 yds. per s/r. Adaptation. Document in Brunschwig Archives (McClelland Collection). No. 10880.06 (pink and green on white).

&. MAIZE. French, 1800–20, block print. 18½″ wide plus 4¼″ border, 22¾″ repeat, 6 yds. per s/r. Document in Brunschwig Archives (McClelland Collection). No. 11399.06 (gray).

&. MAYTIME. French, 1810–25, block print. 28″ wide, 23⅞″ repeat, 5 yds. per s/r. Width reduced by 4″ between stripes. Reproduced for Valentine Museum, Richmond, Va. Document in Brunschwig Archives. No. 10502.06 (gray and orange on blue).

&. MIRAGE. French, 1780–1810, block print. McClelland, p. 137. 27″ wide plus 5¼″ border, 18″ repeat, 5 yds. per s/r. Document at Cooper-Hewitt Museum. No. 12532.06 (blue).

&. ONDINE. French, 1830–35, block print. 21″ wide, 26⅝″ repeat, 6 yds. per s/r. Document at Musée des Arts Décoratifs, Paris. No. 12619.06 (gray).

&. PASSIFLORE. French, 1825–35, block print. 27¾″ wide, 4⅝″ repeat, 5 yds. per s/r. Document at Musée des Arts Décoratifs, Paris. No. 12547.06 (dusty mauve).

&. PENELOPE. American or French, 1810–25, block print. 28″ wide, ⅞″ repeat, 5 yds. per s/r. Slight color change. Reproduced for Liberty Hall, Kenansville, N.C. Document in Brunschwig Archives. No. 792.06 (white on blue).

&. SPATTERWARE. Probably English or French, 1790–1820, block print. 27″ wide, 5 yds. per s/r. Document in Brunschwig Archives. No. 11702.06 (blue).

&. TENTURE FLOTTANTE. French, 1820–40, block print. 20¾″ wide, 21¼″ repeat, 6 yds. per s/r. Adaptation. Document in Brunschwig Archives (McClelland Collection). No. 11569.06 (gray).

&. TRELLIS. French, 1800–05, block print. Nouvel, fig. 166, p. 61. 27″ wide, 3½″ repeat, 5 yds. per s/r. Document at Musée des Arts Décoratifs, Paris. No. 12579.06 (gray).

COLE AND SON

Most of the designs listed are available as special orders. Custom color can be printed.

&. CHINESE TRELLIS. English, 1830–60, block print. Oman and Hamilton, fig. 265, p. 159. 21″ wide, 11 yds. per s/r. No. 98846 (gold on white).

&. CLANDON. English, 1810–20, block print with flock. Oman and Hamilton, fig. 128, p. 128. 21″ wide, 11 yds. per s/r. Reproduction not flocked. No. 98880 (red).

&. FLOWER SPRAY. English, 1790–1810, block print. 21″ wide, 10½″ repeat, 11 yds. per s/r. No. 98883 (tan on white).

PASSIFLORE, 1825–35.
Brunschwig and Fils.
Dusty mauve.

TRELLIS, 1800–05. Brun-
schwig and Fils. Gray.

BRIGHTON, 1780–90.
Katzenbach and Warren.
Red, blue and green on
cream.

&❧ HADDON HALL. English, 1780–1810, block print. 21″ wide, 13″ repeat, 11 yds. per s/r. No. 98840 (brown on white).

&❧ WHICKHAM. English, 1780–1800, block print. 21″ wide, 30″ repeat, 11 yds. per s/r. No. 98831 (green on blue).

A.L. DIAMENT AND COMPANY

&❧ DOROFEE. French, 1835–40, block print. 27″ wide, 10½″ repeat, 5 yds. per s/r. No. 102-19 (beige).

&❧ HERMITAGE SIDEWALL. French, 1830–50, block print. 21¾″ wide, 18½″ repeat, 6 yds. per s/r. No. 111-03 (green and copper).

&❧ MENTON. French, 1815–25, block print. 27″ wide, 18½″ repeat, 5 yds. per s/r. No. 80211-07 (gray).

PHILIP GRAF WALLPAPERS

&❧ CONSUELLA. English, 1790–1810, block print. 27″ wide, 28″ repeat. Outline color not printed. No. 226-1 (white on dark blue).

KATZENBACH AND WARREN

&❧ BRIGHTON. English, 1780–90, block print. 27″ wide, 36″ repeat, 5 yds. per s/r. Document at Colonial Williamsburg. No. 60-0101-5 (red, blue and green on cream).

&❧ DORSET. English or American, 1805–25, block print. 24″ wide, 9¼″ repeat, 6 yds. per s/r. Document at Colonial Williamsburg. No. 60-0198-4 (red on blue). Alternate color: No. 60-0198-1 (white on gold).

&❧ FOX GRAPE. English or French, 1790–1810, block print. 18″ wide, 18¾″ repeat, 8 yds. per s/r. Document at Colonial Williamsburg. No. 60-0021-3 (green and blue on beige).

&❧ HYDE PARK. American, 1825–40, block print. 20″ wide, 19″ repeat, 7 yds. per s/r. Document at Colonial Williamsburg. No. 60-0080-9 (multi on dark brown).

&❧ MADISON. English or French, 1825–40, block print. 21½″ wide, 21″ repeat, 6½ yds. per s/r. Document at Colonial Williamsburg. No. 60-0090-3 (green and yellow on white).

&❧ STENCIL SQUARE. American, 1800–20, block print. 19″ wide, 18⅞″ repeat, 8 yds. per s/r. Document at Colonial Williamsburg. No. 60-0034-4 (blue on beige). Alternate colors: No. 60-0034-2 (gold on white); No. 60-0034-3 (white on green).

&❧ WINDHAM. English or French, 1815–35, block print. 18½″ wide, 21¼″ repeat, 8 yds. per s/r. Document at Colonial Williamsburg. No. 60-0102-9 (gray).

&❧ WINTERBERRY. American, 1810–20, block print. 22″ wide, 5¼″ repeat, 6 yds. per s/r. Document at Colonial Williamsburg. No. 60-0084-1 (yellow ground with red).

&❧ YARMOUTH. American, 1810–25, block print. 18″ wide, 6¾″ repeat, 8 yds. per s/r. Document at Colonial Williamsburg. No. 60-0089-6 (red and white on ochre).

MADISON, 1825–40.
Katzenbach and Warren.
Green and yellow on
white.

FOX GRAPE, 1790–1810.
Katzenbach and Warren.
Green and blue on beige.

STENCIL SQUARE,
1800–20. Katzenbach and
Warren. Blue on beige.

DORSET, 1805–25.
Katzenbach and Warren.
Red and blue.

THE CEDARS, 1830–40. Scalamandré. Pearl gray on pongee.

LEE JOFA

᪥ MEDAILLONS. French, 1780–1800, block print. 27″ wide, 42½″ repeat, 5 yds. per s/r. No. P7011 (blue).*

᪥ NAIROBI. English, 1800–15, block print. 23½″ wide, 13½″ repeat. No. P5419 (brown).*

᪥ PANIER. English or American, 1810–25, block print. 27″ wide, 30″ repeat, 5 yds. per s/r. No. P808253 (topaz). Alternate color: No. P808257 (bamboo).*

᪥ TAIWAN. English, 1780–1800, block print. 27″ wide, 32¼″ repeat, 5 yds. per s/r. No. P5911 (blue).*

SCALAMANDRÉ

᪥ BLAKESLEE HOUSE. American or French, 1830–40, block print. 27⅞″ wide, 22″ repeat, 5 yds. per s/r. Reproduced for Old Economy Village, Ambridge, Pa. No. WP8820-1 (white and brown on blue).

᪥ THE CEDARS. American, 1830–40, block print. Nouvel, fig. 13, p. 134. 18½″ wide, 18⁷⁄₁₆″ repeat, 8 yds. per s/r. Reproduced for Bliss Nash Davis House, Danville, Vt. No. WP81221-1 (pearl gray on pongee).

᪥ CHESTERFIELD. American, 1800–20, block print. 28½″ wide, 6⅞″ repeat, 5 yds. per s/r. Reproduced for Hayes Tavern, Brattleboro, Vt. No. WP8640-1 (brown and white on tan).

BIRDS OF PARADISE,
1780–1810. The Twigs.
Multi.

CHESTERFIELD, 1800–20
Scalamandré. Brown and
white on tan.

48 LAURENS STREET,
1800–20. Scalamandré.
Yellow ground.

☙ CHRISTOPHER MURPHY HOUSE. Probably American, c. 1820, block print. 27″wide. Savannah Collection. No. WP81125-1 (green and white on yellow).

☙ COURTNEY HOUSE. French or English, 1820–35, block print. 27½″ wide, 17½″ repeat. Old Deerfield Collection. No. WP8909-26 (white and gray on blue). Special order.

☙ DERBY HOUSE. American, 1800–20, block print. 26¾″wide, 8¾″ repeat, 5 yds. per s/r. Document at Shelburne Museum, Shelburne, Vt. No. WP8931-1 (yellow and green on white).

☙ FARRINGTON HOUSE. Probably American, 1815–30, block print. 28″ wide, 10″ repeat, 5 yds. per s/r. Adaptation. Old Deerfield Collection. No. 8902-25 (white and green on light blue). Alternate colors: No. 8902-28 (lilac on white); No. 8902-29 (white on yellow).

☙ 48 LAURENS STREET. English, 1800–10, block print. 27″ wide, 36″ repeat, 5 yds. per s/r. Historic Charleston Reproductions. No. WP81274-1 (blue ground). Alternate color: No. WP81274-2 (yellow ground).

☙ HAYES TAVERN. French or English, 1810–25, block print. 28½″ wide, 8″ repeat, 5 yds. per s/r. Reproduced for Hayes Tavern, Brattleboro, Vt. No. WP8642-1 (blue and white on gray).

☙ MUIR'S MEDALLION. French or American, 1830–40, block print. 27″ wide, 15½″ repeat, 5 yds. per s/r. Old Deerfield Collection. No. WP8913-25 (blue on gold).

☙ PRINCESS LACE. American, 1810–25, block print. 27½″wide, 20″ repeat. Old Deerfield Collection. No. WP8905-25 (cream on beige). Special order.

THE TWIGS

☙ BIRDS OF PARADISE. French, 1780–1810, block print. McClelland, p. 244. 18″ wide, 37″ repeat. Adaptation. Reproduced for Gore Place, Waltham, Mass. No. 6504 (multi); No. 6501 (multi).

☙ DRAPERY SIDEWALL. French, 1810–25, block print. 27½″ wide, 23⅜″ repeat, 5 yds. per s/r. No. 5501 (gray).

☙ DUTTON HOUSE. American, 1810–25, block print. 27″ wide, 5″ repeat. No. A-221-7 (white on beige); No. A-221-6 (white on cream).

☙ FOLSOM TAVERN. French, 1835–45, block print. 27″ wide, 12″ repeat. No. A-202-12 (tan).

☙ JAFFREY ROOM. French, 1780–90, block print. 22½″ wide, 42½″repeat. Document at Museum of Fine Arts, Boston. No. 4010 (multi on white).

☙ JEWETT HOUSE. American, 1800–10, block print. 27″ wide, 9″ repeat. No. A-209-10 (gray on white); No. A-209-6 (blue on white).

☙ KNAPP HOUSE. French, 1810–20, block print. 19″ wide, 23½″ repeat. No. A-156-5 (peach and green). Alternate color: No. A-156-3 (tan and green).

☙ LA NANCY. French, 1810–20, block print. 19″ wide, 22½″ repeat. No. A-229-9 (gold); No. A-229-4 (white).

ર્ટ્ LEAVES. French, 1810—25, block print. 21½″ wide, 31¼″ repeat, 7 yds. per s/r. No. A-286-5 (gray and green); No. A-286-8 (brown and orange); No. A-286-4 (tan).

ર્ટ્ LINKS CLUB. American. 1810—20, block print. 27½″ wide, 9″ repeat. No. A-115-9 (orange and green on white).

ર્ટ્ THIMBLEBERRY. American, 1780—1800, block print. 26½″ wide, 3½″ repeat. Original color not reproduced. Alternate color: No. A-167-9 (brown and black on white).

WATERHOUSE WALLHANGINGS

ર્ટ્ BREWSTER FLORAL. Probably American, 1800—20, block print. 20½″ wide, 15½″ repeat, 7 yds. per s/r. Document in Waterhouse Archives. No. 194635 (slate blue on white).

ર્ટ્ CHATHAM LACE. Probably American, 1825—35, block print. 20″ wide, 9½″ repeat, 7 yds. per s/r. Document in Waterhouse Archives. No. 190312 (blue). Alternate colors: No. 190335 (pink); No. 190519 (gray); No. 190518 (yellow).

ર્ટ્ CHRISTMAS ROSE. Probably American, 1790—1810, block print. 24″ wide, 2½″ repeat, 6 yds. per s/r. Original color not reproduced. Document in Waterhouse Archives. Alternate color: No. 161258 (green on light blue).

ર્ટ્ COYLE HOUSE. American, 1822—28, block print. Lynn, figs. 12—19 and 12—20, p. 283. 26½″ wide, 5 yds. per s/r. Document at Old Sturbridge Village, Sturbridge, Mass., and Coyle House, Natchez, Miss. No. 168190 (pink and white on yellow). Alternate color: No. 168579 (green and orange on light green).

ર્ટ્ DANDELION STRIPE. American, 1810—25, block print. 18″ wide, 7 yds. per s/r. Document in Waterhouse Archives. No. 128512 (blue and orange). Alternate colors: No. 128622 (mustard); No. 128518 (yellow).

ર્ટ્ DEVIL PAPER. French, 1820—40, block print. 26½″ wide, 5 yds. per s/r. Document at Gore Place, Waltham, Mass. No. 138576 (black on white).

ર્ટ્ EAGLE HILL. English, 1790—1810, block print. 26″ wide, 4½″ repeat, 5 yds. per s/r. Color not reproduced exactly. Document in Waterhouse Archives. No. 106335 (gray on white).

ર્ટ્ EDGARTOWN. American, 1800—15, block print. 23¾″ wide, 9½″ repeat, 6 yds. per s/r. Document in Waterhouse Archives. No. 163618 (brown ground).

ર્ટ્ ENOCH FRYE. Probably American, 1790—1810, block print. 24″ wide, 9½″ repeat, 7 yds. per s/r. Document in Waterhouse Archives. Sample at Society for the Preservation of New England Antiquities. No. 112815 (ochre on gray-green). Alternate color: No. 112496 (white on blue).

ર્ટ્ FRENCH TASSEL. French or American, 1810—25, block print. 21½″ wide, 15½″ repeat, 7 yds. per s/r. Sample at Society for the Preservation of New England Antiquities. No. 123437 (blue ground).

CHATHAM LACE,
1825–35. Waterhouse
Wallhangings. Blue.

ENOCH FRYE,
1790–1810. Waterhouse
Wallhangings. Ochre
on gray-green.

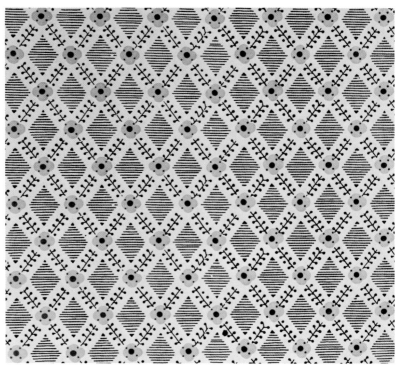

COYLE HOUSE, 1822–28.
Waterhouse Wallhangings.
Pink and white on yellow.

FRENCH TASSEL,
1810–25. Waterhouse
Wallhangings. Blue
ground.

BREWSTER FLORAL,
1800–20. Waterhouse
Wallhangings. Slate blue
on white.

❧ THE GAZEBO. French, 1790–1800, block print. 20½" wide, 22" repeat, 7 yds. per s/r. Document in Waterhouse Archives. No. 186613 (red and blue on gray). Alternate color: No. 186444 (pink and green on blue).

❧ GENERAL JOHN WALKER. American, 1790–1810, block print. 20½" wide, 5½" repeat, 7 yds. per s/r. Document in Waterhouse Archives. No. 188437 (white and black on blue).

❧ GENERAL THAYER. American, 1780–1810, block print. 19" wide, 7 yds. per s/r. Reproduced for Sylvanus Thayer House, Braintree, Mass. Sample at Society for the Preservation of New England Antiquities. No. 117840 (red ground).

❧ GORE PLACE. French, 1780–1810, block print. 18¾" wide, 19" repeat, 7 yds. per s/r. Document at Gore Place, Waltham, Mass. No. 139506 (multi on beige).

❧ GOVERNOR BADGER. American or French, 1815–30, block print. 18" wide, 19" repeat, 7 yds. per s/r. Document in Waterhouse Archives. No. 113426 (red on brown). Alternate color: No. 113496 (orange on blue).

❧ LE PECHEUR. French, 1790–1810, block print. 18¾" wide, 18¾" repeat, 7 yds. per s/r. Document in Waterhouse Archives. No. 175206 (blue and orange on white).

❧ LOUISE. French or American, 1810–30, block print. 27" wide, 18½" repeat, 5 yds. per s/r. Document in Waterhouse Archives. No. 141447 (pink and green on ochre). Alternate color: No. 141581 (green on gray).

❧ MARY LYON. French or American, 1810–20, block print. 28" wide, 5 yds. per s/r. Document in Waterhouse Archives. No. 136632 (pink).

❧ MEDALLION. French, 1820–30, block print. 28¼" wide, 7" repeat, 5 yds. per s/r. Document in Waterhouse Archives. No. 104613 (yellow on gray).

❧ NORWELL STRIPE. American, 1810–20, block print. 26" wide, 5½" repeat, 5 yds. per s/r. Document in Waterhouse Archives. No. 108463 (rust on tan).

❧ NYE HOMESTEAD. American, 1790–1810, block print. 26½" wide, 5 yds. per s/r. Document in Waterhouse Archives. No. 118496 (white on blue).

❧ PARKER HILL. American, 1825–35, block print. 19" wide, 18½" repeat. Document in Waterhouse Archives. Alternate color: No. 114650 (tan ground).

❧ PENOBSCOT. English or American, 1800–15, block print. 24" wide, 7 yds. per s/r. Document in Waterhouse Archives. No. 156202 (blue on brown ground).

❧ PLYMOUTH STENCIL. American, 1815–35, block print. 20" wide, 9½" repeat, 7 yds. per s/r. Document in Waterhouse Archives. No. 191613 (blue on light gray).

GENERAL JOHN
WALKER, 1790–1810.
Waterhouse Wallhangings.
White and black on blue.

GORE PLACE, 1780–1810.
Waterhouse Wallhangings.
Multi on beige.

LOUISE, 1810–30.
Waterhouse Wallhangings.
Pink and green on ochre.

NYE HOMESTEAD,
1790–1810. Waterhouse
Wallhangings. White on
blue.

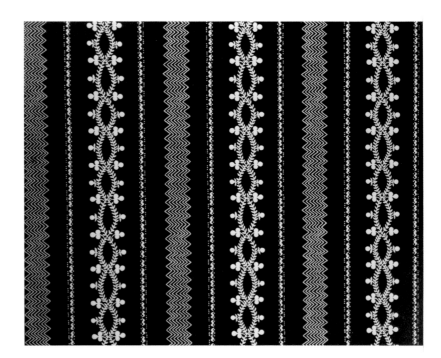

SALEM STRIPE, 1790–1815. Waterhouse Wall-hangings. White on blue.

❧ SALEM STRIPE. Probably American, 1790–1815, block print. 26½″ wide, 5 yds. per s/r. Document in Waterhouse Archives. No. 169437 (white on blue).

❧ STRAWBERRY STRIPE. American, 1810–25, block print. 24″ wide, 7 yds. per s/r. Document in Waterhouse Archives. No. 143447 (mustard).

❧ STRAWBERY BANKE STENCIL. American, 1815–25, block print. 24¼″ wide, 21″ repeat, 7 yds. per s/r. Document at Strawbery Banke, Portsmouth, N.H. No. 145158 (blue on mustard).

❧ WHEAT DAMASK. American, 1810–25, block print. 24″ wide, 24″ repeat, 7 yds. per s/r. Document in Waterhouse Archives. No. 154590 (green on blue).

WAVERLY

❧ CHARLTON STRIPE. American, 1810–25, block print. 20½″ wide, 5⅛″ repeat, 7 yds. per s/r. Document at Old Sturbridge Village, Sturbridge, Mass. No. 4324-A (document gold).

❧ STURBRIDGE BASKETWEAVE. American, 1810–25, block print. 20½″ wide, 5⅛″ repeat, 7 yds. per s/r. Document at Old Sturbridge Village, Sturbridge, Mass. No. 4335-A (blue). Alternate colors: No. 4335-B (natural); No. 4335-C (claypot).

❧ TOWNE HOUSE FLORAL STRIPE. American or French, 1825–40, block print. 20½″ wide, 16″ repeat, 7 yds. per s/r. Document at Old Sturbridge Village, Sturbridge, Mass. No. 3917-A (leaf green).

LOUIS W. BOWEN   BORDERS

ે VERSAILLES BORDERS (architectural elements). French, 1800–25, block print. Charcoal tones, gray, white.*

 GUILLOCHE. 3½" wide, 9" repeat. No. 87004-A.
 DOUBLE GREEK WAVE. 3" wide, 9¼" repeat. No. 87004-B.
 EGG AND DART. 4⁷⁄₁₆" wide, 9" repeat. No. 87004-C.
 COLUMN. 3¼" wide, 16¾" repeat. No. 87004-D.
 SPIRAL. 5¼" wide, 36" repeat. No. 87004-E.
 LEAF AND SPIRAL. 2½" wide, 17¾" repeat. No. 87004-F.
 CORNICE. 12½" wide, 19" repeat. No. 87004-G.

BRUNSCHWIG AND FILS

ે ASHLAR BORDER NO. 1. American, 1800–10, block print. 4½" wide, 18¼" repeat. Adaptation. Reproduced for Boscobel, Garrison-on-Hudson, N.Y. No. 11358.06 (tan).

ે BOSPHORE BORDER. French, 1810–25, block print. 9¾" wide, 18½" repeat. Document in Brunschwig Archives (McClelland Collection). No. 11541.06 (red and green). Alternate color: No. 11542.06 (blue and green).

ે BOSPHORE TASSEL BORDER. French, 1810–25, block print. 3¾" wide, 18⅛" repeat. Document in Brunschwig Archives (McClelland Collection). No. 11551.06 (red and green). Alternate color: No. 11552.06 (blue and green).

ે BRAINTREE ACORN BORDER. American, 1800–10, block print. 3¾" wide, 20" repeat. Document at Society for the Preservation of New England Antiquities. No. 11076.06 (terra cotta).

ે PATCHWORK BORDER. French, 1800–20, block print. Lynn, p. 131. 4⅝" wide, 4⅝" repeat. Document at Cooper-Hewitt Museum. No. 12442.06 (multi with pink and sky blue).

ે PLIAGE BORDER. French, 1825–50, block print. 4½" wide, 2¼" repeat. Document at Musée des Arts Décoratifs, Paris. No. 12559.06 (gray).

ે PORTSMOUTH DAISY BORDER. English, 1800–10, block print with flocking. 5½" wide, 20" repeat. Reproduction not flocked. Document at Society for the Preservation of New England Antiquities. No. 11086.06 (terra cotta).

ે SALEM FEATHER BORDER. American, 1790–1810, block print. 2¾" wide, 20" repeat. Document at Society for the Preservation of New England Antiquities. No. 11096.06 (terra cotta).

ે SUDBURY PINEAPPLE BORDER. English or American, 1790–1810, block print. 3¾" wide, 20" repeat. Document at Society for the Preservation of New England Antiquities. No. 11066.06 (terra cotta).

A.L. DIAMENT AND COMPANY

ે HERMITAGE LION BORDER. French, 1830–50, block print. 9¾" wide, 21½" repeat. No. 110-03 (green and copper).

BOSPHORE BORDER, 1810—25. Brunschwig and Fils. Blue and green.

PATCHWORK BORDER, 1800—20. Brunschwig and Fils. Multi with pink and sky blue.

BRAINTREE ACORN BORDER, 1800—10. Brunschwig and Fils. Terra cotta.

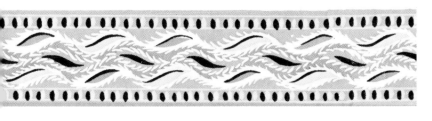

SALEM FEATHER BORDER, 1790—1810. Brunschwig and Fils. Terra cotta.

SUDBURY PINEAPPLE BORDER, 1790—1810. Brunschwig and Fils. Terra cotta.

CHARLESTON FRIEZE,
1800–25. Scalamandré.
Pink and green.

STROBEL FRIEZE,
1810–30. Scalamandré.
White and gold on green.

PLIAGE BORDER, 1825–50.
Brunschwig and Fils. Gray.

PORTSMOUTH DAISY
BORDER, 1800–10.
Brunschwig and Fils.
Terra cotta.

SCALAMANDRÉ

✿ CHARLESTON FRIEZE. French, 1800–25, block print. 6½" wide, 18" repeat. Historic Charleston Reproductions. No. WPBD81268-1 (pink and green).

✿ 48 LAURENS STREET FRET. Probably English, 1800–10, block print. 1⅜" wide, ¾" repeat. Adaptation. Historic Charleston Reproductions. No. WPBD81275-1 (blue ground).

✿ STROBEL FRIEZE. French, 1810–30, block print. 6¾" wide, 18" repeat. Historic Charleston Reproductions. No. WPBD81271-1 (white and gold on green).

THE TWIGS

✿ CONCORD BORDER. American, 1810–25, block print. 5½" wide, 5½" repeat. Original color not reproduced. Alternate color: No. 6604 (red and tan).

✿ FLEURETTE FRIEZE. French, 1810–15, block print. 9" wide, 19" repeat. No. A165-1 (tan).

✿ LA NANCY FRIEZE AND BASE BORDER. French, 1810–20, block print. Frieze 13½"; border 5¼", 19¼" repeat. No. A231-9 (pink and green on tan).

WAVERLY

✿ STURBRIDGE BORDER. French, 1810–25, block print. 3½" wide, 12½" repeat. Document at Old Sturbridge Village, Sturbridge, Mass. No. 3916-A (ebony).

PLAIN PAPERS

SCALAMANDRÉ

Plain papers that approximate the popular colors of the late 18th and early 19th centuries include the following ground papers, 30" wide: No. 146 (smoke blue); No. 357 (pastel citron); No. 363 (hydrangea pink); No. 364 (powder blue); No. 396 (empire blue); No. 410 (sage); No. 462 (ecru); No. 1852 (blue sky); No. 1855 (rouge).

SCENIC PAPERS

A. L. DIAMENT AND COMPANY

The French scenic wallpapers listed are either silk-screen reproductions or reprints from the original blocks. A. L. Diament also carries complete or partial sets of original French scenic wallpapers. The titles given to the reproductions are not necessarily those of the original papers. In some cases, two or more modern sets have been made by dividing an original set. For example, "Natural Wonders" and "Review" were originally part of "Scenic America."

✿ BANKS OF THE BOSPHORUS. French, 1832, block print. McClelland, p. 365. 6½' per set, 39" per strip, 2 strips per set. No. 20030-013 (multi).

✿ BRANDYWINE HUNDRED. French, 1831 and 1852, block print. 42¾' per set, 28½" per strip, 18 strips per set. No. 20040-013 (multi).

COROMANDEL COAST, 1806. A.L. Diament. Multi.

❧ CARNIVAL OF PEGASUS. French, 1837, block print. 39'7" per set, 19" per strip, 25 strips per set. No. 20095-007 (gray).

❧ THE CHASE. French, 1831, block print. 28½' per set, 28½" per strip, 12 strips per set. No. 20038 (gray).

❧ CLASSICAL LANDSCAPE. French, 1825, block print. 10½' per set, 21" per strip, 6 strips per set. No. 20006-007 (gray on gray).

❧ COAST OF MALABAR. French, 1806, block print. 15'5½" per set, 26½" per strip, 7 strips per set. No. 20102-013 (multi).

❧ COROMANDEL COAST. French, 1806, block print. 15'5½" per set, 26½" per strip, 7 strips per set. No. 20106-013 (multi).

❧ FESTIVAL OF ROME. French, 1837, block print. 31'8" per set, 19" per strip, 20 strips per set. No. 20094-007 (gray).

❧ FIRST MEETING OF THE SEASON. French, 1837, block print. 30'1" per set, 19" per strip, 19 strips per set. No. 20093-007 (gray).

❧ GENTLEMEN'S SPORT. French, 1831, block print. 28½' per set, 18" per strip, 19 strips per set. No. 20046-013 (multi).

❧ HORSE RACING. French, 1837, block print. 50'8" per set, 19" per strip, 32 strips per set. No. 20011-007 (gray).

❧ HUNTING (Set 4). French, 1831, block print. 28" per strip, 6 strips per set. No. 20088-013 (multi).

❧ LANDSCAPE. French, 1831, block print. 14¼' per set, 28½" per strip, 6 strips per set. No. 20035-007 (gray).

❧ MONTCHANIN. French, 1831, block print. 14¼' per set, 28½" per strip, 6 strips per set. No. 20037-013 (multi).

❧ NATURAL WONDERS. French, 1834, block print. McClelland, p. 387, part of "Scenic America." 13½' per set, 18" per strip, 9 strips per set. No. 20051-013 (multi).

❧ PICNIC. French, 1831, block print. 15' per set, 18" per strip, 10 strips per set. No. 20043-013 (multi).

PROMENADE. French, 1834, block print. 10½' per set, 18" per strip, 7 strips per set. No. 20048-013 (multi).

REVIEW. French, 1834, block print. McClelland, p. 387, part of "Scenic America." 10½' per set, 18" per strip, 7 strips per set. No. 20049-013 (multi).

ROMAN HORSE RACE. French, 1837, block print. 20'7" per set, 19" per strip, 13 strips per set. No. 20099-007 (gray).

STEEPLE-CHASE. French, 1837, block print. 11'1" per strip, 7 strips per set. No. 20097-007 (gray).

THOROUGHBRED RACE AND PUBLIC CARRIAGE. French, 1837, block print. McClelland, p. 293. 19' per set, 19" per strip, 12 strips per set. No. 20098-007 (gray).

VALLEY FORGE. French, 1831 and 1852, block print. 14¼' per set, 28½" per strip, 6 strips per set. No. 20036-007 (multi).

WAR OF INDEPENDENCE. French, 1831 and 1852, block print. 28½' per set, 28½" per strip, 12 strips per set. No. 20039-007 (multi).

WILD BOAR. French, 1831, block print. 9' per set, 18" per strip, 6 strips per set. No. 20044-013 (multi).

WILD DUCK. French, 1831, block print. 13½' per set, 18" per strip, 9 strips per set. No. 20042-013 (multi).

THE TWIGS

THE MONUMENTS OF PARIS. French, 1814, block print. 48' per set, 17"–28" per panel, 22 panels per set. 8½' high. Half set (11 panels) and quartet (4 panels) available. Complete set also available at 15' high. Reproduced in cooperation with Metropolitan Museum of Art.

WILD BOAR, 1831.
A.L. Diament. Multi.

1840 TO 1870:
REVIVAL STYLES AND
MACHINE PRINTING

The changes brought on by the Industrial Revolution were more clearly evident in the wallpaper industry after 1840. The production of wallpaper by machine had an impact on the product itself as well as on the appearance of American interiors. The colors used in machine printing were thinner than those used in block printing, thus giving a different visual effect to the design. The circumference of the printing roller imposed tight restrictions on the size of the repeat. Paper width became standardized. The machine enabled manufacturers to produce larger quantities of wallpaper, making it less expensive and more readily available to the general population.

During this period an increasing number of books and magazines were being published on how to decorate and manage the home. They promoted the use of wallpaper and began to codify patterns for specific rooms. For example, papers imitating stone, such as "Carrara" (page 68), were recommended for hallways.

The mid-19th century marked the beginning of an age of revival styles. Wallpaper manufacturers were quick to create designs that would be compatible with any style or whim of fashion. The two dominant styles during this 30-year period were the Gothic Revival and the Rococo Revival. Andrew Jackson Downing, a great promoter of the Gothic Revival style in architecture, approved of wallpaper as an appropriate treatment for the walls. However, he preferred floral designs and papers in imitation wood grain instead of Gothic Revival papers with designs imitating pointed, carved stone arches. Evidence suggests that the latter were used to lend an air of fashion in redecorating old buildings.

Bold scrolls and combinations of flowers and scrolls epitomize Rococo Revival papers. These were produced in an endless variety of design and quality, making them affordable for use in almost any building. A representative example is "Eastman" (page 74). Striped papers and those with small repeating patterns often incorporated Gothic or Rococo elements. "Belle Epoch" (page 75) is a reproduction of a simple style of paper that coexisted with the proliferation of patterns; it was used extensively in the 1860s. Its elegant effect was achieved by laying gold leaf over a design embossed on a highly polished ground.

MONCEAU, 1855–60.
Brunschwig and Fils.
Aubergine.

CARRARA, 1860–70.
Brunschwig and Fils.
Gold.

BACHELOR'S BUTTON,
1862. Bradbury and Brad-
bury.

By the early 1870s, a reaction built against the elaborate and overornamented French papers that had been so popular. This movement was led by English theorists who analyzed wallpaper design and imposed moral attitudes on it. They maintained that wallpaper should be "honest" and should not attempt to make a flat wall appear three-dimensional. These contrasting principles of design are illustrated by comparing "Mignonne," a French paper (page 71), and "Isis," an English paper (page 75).

The designs favored during the mid-19th century apparently do not hold the same appeal for the 20th-century eye, and few reproductions of the most popular types of patterns from this period are available today.

BRADBURY AND BRADBURY

WALLPAPERS

In addition to reproductions of historic wallpapers, Bradbury and Bradbury offers adaptations of wallpapers and wall treatments derived from design books published in the late 19th century. Most Bradbury and Bradbury papers are available in four period colorways created according to late 19th-century color theory. Only document colors are listed. Bradbury and Bradbury papers are ordered by pattern name and color.

ઢ BACHELOR'S BUTTON. English, 1862. 27″ wide, 7″ repeat, 5 yds. per s/r. Adaptation of a published design by Christopher Dresser.

ઢ CARPENTER GOTHIC. American, 1860–70, machine print. 25″ wide, 19″ repeat, 5 yds. per s/r. Reproduced for Lathrop House, Redwood City, Calif. Crimson and vert on buff.

ઢ FAIR OAKS. English, 1850–60, block print. Oman and Hamilton, fig. 268, p. 160. 27″ wide, 7″ repeat, 13% reduction in scale. Document at Victoria and Albert Museum.

ઢ FLEUR DE LYS. English, 1840–50, block print. 27″ wide, 7″ repeat, 5 yds. per s/r. ¼ scale of original design by Pugin. Document at Victoria and Albert Museum. Gold on buff.

ઢ WIDOW CLARK STRIPE. American or French, 1850–60, machine print. 18½″ wide, 18⅝″ repeat, 23 square feet per s/r. Reproduced for Chicago Architectural Foundation et al. Document at Chicago Historical Society. Blue and gray.

BRUNSCHWIG AND FILS

ઢ CARRARA. American, 1860–70, machine print. 28″ wide, 18″ repeat. Document at Cooper-Hewitt Museum. No. 12523.06 (gold).

ઢ ELVIRE SIDEWALL. French, 1840–60, block print. Greysmith, fig. 89, p. 120. 27″ wide, 3½″ repeat, 5 yds. per s/r. No. 10260.06 (red and blue). Alternate color: No. 10262.06 (blue and brown).

ઢ MIGNONNE. French, 1850–60, block print. Nouvel, fig. 222, p. 69. 24″ wide, 24″ repeat, 5 yds. per s/r. Document at Musée des Arts Décoratifs, Paris. No. 12639.06 (gray).

ઢ MONCEAU. French, 1855–60, block print. 17¾″ wide, 21½″ repeat, 7 yds. per s/r. Adaptation. Document at Musée des Arts Décoratifs, Paris. No. 12677.06 (aubergine).

WIDOW CLARK STRIPE, 1850–60. Bradbury and Bradbury. Blue and gray.

CARPENTER GOTHIC, 1860–70. Bradbury and Bradbury. Crimson and vert on buff.

STRAWBERRY, 1850.
Cole and Son. White
ground.

MIGNONNE, 1850–60.
Brunschwig and Fils. Gray.

NOWTON COURT, 1840–50. Cole and Son. Rose and brown.

COLE AND SON

Most of the designs listed are available as special orders. Custom color can be printed.

❧ BUTTERFIELD TILE. English, 1860–70, machine print. 21″ wide, 11 yds. per s/r. No. 98859 (tan and brown).

❧ CHINESE FRET. English, 1850–60, machine print. 21″ wide, 11 yds. per s/r. No. 98849 (white on green).

❧ CRACE DIAPER. English, c. 1848, block print. Oman and Hamilton, fig. 1116, p. 403. 21″ wide, 11 yds. per s/r. No. 98855 (light olive on white).

❧ CRACE TILE. English, 1850–60, machine print. 21″ wide, 10½″ repeat, 11 yds. per s/r. No. 98860 (terra cotta and brown).

❧ GOTHIC LILY. English, c. 1850, block print. 21″ wide, 16″ repeat, 11 yds. per s/r. No. 98862 (white ground). Alternate color: No. 98863 (brown ground).

❧ NOWTON COURT. English, 1840–50, block print and flock. Oman and Hamilton, fig. 533, p. 204. 21″ wide, 10½″ repeat, 11 yds. per s/r. Reproduction not flocked. No. 98866 (rose and brown).

❧ QUATREFOIL. English, 1850–60. 21″ wide, 11 yds. per s/r. No. 98853 (tan on white).

❧ SMALL GOTHIC SCREEN. English, 1840–60, machine print. 21″ wide, 7″ repeat, 11 yds. per s/r. No. 98851 (brown on red). Alternate color: No. 98852 (brown on blue).

BUTTERFIELD TILE, 1860–70. Cole and Son. Tan and brown.

ᛣ STRAWBERRY. English, c. 1850, block print. 21″wide, 15″repeat, 11 yds. per s/r. No. 98864 (white ground).

ᛣ VAUGHAN DESIGN. English, 1860–70, machine print. 21″ wide, 5″repeat, 11 yds. per s/r. No. OEW166 (gold and brown).

COWTAN AND TOUT

ᛣ FUSCIA. English, 1860–70, block print. 21″wide, 21″repeat. No. 20100 (multi with gold stripe).*

LEE JOFA

ᛣ HOLLYHOCK MINOR. French, 1840–50, block print. 24″wide with 3½″border, 23½″repeat, 5 yds. per s/r. No. P9394-0 (cream). Alternate color: No. P9395-0 (light green).*

SCALAMANDRÉ

ᛣ AMES VINE AND FRET. American or French, 1840–60, machine print. 27″ wide, 18¼″ repeat, 5 yds. per s/r. Old Deerfield Collection. No. WP8912-25 (green and white on gray).

ᛣ EASTMAN. French or American, 1840–50, machine print. 23⅜″ wide, 20⅜″ repeat, 6 yds. per s/r. Reproduced for George Eastman Birthplace, Rochester, N.Y. No. WP81188-1 (green and white on gray).

ᛣ KELTON HOUSE RESTORATION. American, 1860–75, machine print. 18½″ wide, 19½″ repeat, 7 yds. per s/r. Reproduced for Kelton

EASTMAN, 1840–50.
Scalamandré. Green and
white on gray.

ISIS, 1865–75. Waterhouse
Wallhangings. Green and
red on blue.

BELLE EPOCH, 1860–70.
Waterhouse Wallhangings.
Gold on gray.

House, Columbus, Ohio. No.WP81202-1 (red and green on brown).

&❧ LOCUST GROVE FLOWER. Probably English, 1850–60, machine print. 18¾" wide, 1⅞" repeat, 8 yds. per s/r. Reproduced for Young-Morse Historic Site, Poughkeepsie, N.Y. No. WP81227-1 (gray on white).

&❧ PITTSON HOUSE. American or English, 1840–50, machine print. 28" wide, 22" repeat, 5 yds. per s/r. Reproduced for Old Economy Village, Ambridge, Pa. No.WP8788-1 (white and black on gray).

&❧ TOOMBS HOUSE. English, 1850–70, machine print. 18½" wide, 9¼" repeat, 8 yds. per s/r. Reproduced for General Robert Toombs House, Washington, Ga. No.WP81246-1 (gray and gold).

&❧ WAYNE HOUSE. American, 1850–60, machine print. 28" wide, 10" repeat, 5 yds. per s/r. Reproduced for Old Economy Village, Ambridge, Pa. No.WP8821-1 (brown, blue and green on tan).

SCHUMACHER

&❧ CORABELLE. American or French, 1850–60, machine print. 20½" wide, 25" repeat, 7 yds. per s/r. Adaptation; striped paper created from border document. Document in Dornsife Collection, The Victorian Society in America. No.3831A (document multi).

&❧ FEATHER. American, 1840–60, machine print. 20½" wide, 5⅞" repeat, 7 yds. per s/r. Document at Schumacher Museum. No.3849A (document gray).

&❧ MELINDA. American, 1850–60, machine print. 27" wide, 8½" repeat, 5 yds. per s/r. Document in Dornsife Collection, The Victorian Society in America. No.3839A (document blue).

&❧ QUATRAFOIL. American, 1850–70, machine print. 20½" wide, 5⅛" repeat, 7 yds. per s/r. Document at Schumacher Museum. No. 3847A (document porcelain). Alternate color: No.3847D (slate blue).

&❧ RIBBONETTE. American, 1840–60, machine print. 20½" wide, 10¼" repeat, 7 yds. per s/r. Document in Dornsife Collection, The Victorian Society in America. No.3854A (document blue).

WATERHOUSE WALLHANGINGS

&❧ BELLE EPOCH. Probably German, 1860–70, machine print. 27" wide, 12" repeat, 5 yds. per s/r. Document in Waterhouse Archives. No. 183613 (gold on gray). Alternate color: No.183610 (gold on white).

&❧ BISSELL HOUSE. Probably English, 1850–60, machine print. 26½" wide, 5 yds. per s/r. Document at Bissell House, St. Louis, Mo. No. 134467 (gold on white).

&❧ ISIS. English, 1865–75, machine print. 27" wide, 24½" repeat, 5 yds. per s/r. Document in Waterhouse Archives. No.178443 (green and red on blue). Alternate color: No.178700 (blue and red on tan).

&❧ TRELLIS. American or French, 1860–70, machine print. 21" wide, 11" repeat, 7 yds. per s/r. Document in Waterhouse Archives. No. 181335 (pink and green on white).

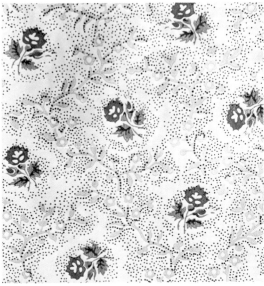

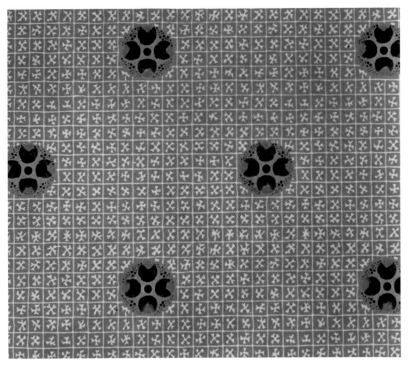

top left
KELTON HOUSE RES-
TORATION, 1860—75.
Scalamandré. Red and
green on brown.

top right
MELINDA, 1850—60.
Schumacher. Document
blue.

left
QUATREFOIL, 1850—70.
Schumacher. Document
porcelain.

VICTORIAN FLORAL,
1860–70. Waterhouse
Wallhangings. Gold on
light gray.

ð VICTORIAN FLORAL. German or English, 1860–70, machine print. 27″ wide, 8½″ repeat, 5 yds. per s/r. Document in Waterhouse Archives. No. 179613 (gold on light gray). Alternate color: No. 179610 (gold on white).

BRUNSCHWIG AND FILS

ð ELVIRE BORDER NO. 1. French, 1840–60, block print. Greysmith, fig. 89, p. 120. 13″ wide, 18¾″ repeat. No. 10270.06 (red and blue). Alternate colors: No. 10272.06 (blue and brown); No. 10274.06 (red and green).

ð ELVIRE BORDER NO. 2. French, 1840–60, block print. Greysmith, fig. 89, p. 120. 5⅜″ wide, 18¾″ repeat. No. 10280.06 (red and blue). Alternate colors: No. 10282.06 (brown and blue); No. 10284.06 (red and green).

COWTAN AND TOUT

ð FUSCHIA CROWN. English, 1860–70, block print. No. CT-20101 (multi with gold stripe).*

SCALAMANDRÉ

ð FLORAL RIBBON AND BEAD BORDER. English or French, 1860–80, machine print. 2½″ wide, 3¾″ repeat. Reproduced for Old Economy Village, Ambridge, Pa. No. BD-400-1 (pink and black).

ð LOCUST GROVE BORDER. English, 1850–60, machine print. 4¾″ wide, ⁷⁄₁₆″ repeat. Reproduced for Young-Morse Historic Site, Poughkeepsie, N.Y. No. WPBD81228-1 (gold and gray).

SCHUMACHER

ð BAROQUE BORDER. French, 1850–70, block print. 3¼″ wide, 4¾″ repeat. Document in Dornsife Collection, The Victorian Society in America. No. 5703A (mulberry and spruce). Alternate color: No. 5703G (sable and dark blue).

ð BAROQUE CORNER. French, 1850–70, block print. Document in Dornsife Collection, The Victorian Society in America. No. 5704A (mulberry and spruce). Alternate color: No. 5704G (sable and dark blue).

ð BRAID BORDER. French, 1840–70, block print. 3¼″ wide, 1½″ repeat. Document in Dornsife Collection, The Victorian Society in America. No. 5706A (document brown and blue).

ð ROPE BORDER. English or American, 1850–60, block print. 1⁵⁄₁₆″ wide, 8″ repeat. Document in Dornsife Collection, The Victorian Society in America. No. 5707A (document cerise and green).

ð SPIRAL BORDER. French, 1840–60, block print. ⅝″ wide, 1″ repeat. Document in Dornsife Collection, The Victorian Society in America. No. 5705A (document rose).

1870 TO 1910:
STYLIZED DESIGNS
FOR THE LATE VICTORIAN ERA

The late 19th century was unparalled in the manufacture and use of wallpaper. Most residential rooms were papered, including kitchens, closets, attic staircases and even privies. Ceilings covered with one or more patterns were also fashionable.

Wallpaper was no longer considered only a finish; it became an essential part of the overall design of a room. Wallpaper design now stood on its own and did not have to imitate other materials such as draped fabric or stone. Books on decorating and pamphlets produced by wallpaper companies promoted the stylized patterns and pale palettes favored by the English design theorists. As a result, England, replacing France, once again became the source for fashionable wallpaper.

Wallpaper manufacturers in England now hired well-known designers and artists to create new patterns. One of the most influential was William Morris, an English designer whose patterns of stylized flowers and foliage caught the eye of Americans. His wallpapers became so popular that they continued to be produced into the 20th century; many of his designs are still appealing and are available as reproductions. Because papers designed by William Morris were expensive, they were not used as extensively in this country as one might expect. His style of design, however, was widely copied, and most Americans had to settle for an inexpensive imitation "Morris paper."

Dividing a wall surface into three horizontal units — frieze, fill and dado — was a popular wall treatment in the 1870s and 1880s. The "Beresford" group (pages 102–04) reproduces this effect; borders mark the division between the different but compatible patterns. Ceilings also could contain one or more different patterns separated by a judicious use of borders. "Bachelor's Pear Vine" (page 107), "Hanger House Garden" (page 108) and "Hanger House" (page 109) were used together to create a patterned ceiling.

The interest in Japanese design is evident in wallpapers produced during the 1880s. The asymmetrical designs and depiction of Japanese figures on papers in the "Anglo-Japanese" style are direct contrasts to the papers being imported from Japan at the same time. See, for example, "Jonesboro" (page 80) and "Mareiko" (page 84). Expensive Japanese

JONESBORO, 1880–90. Richard E. Thibaut. Multi on white.

81

papers emulated the stylized English tradition and were embossed and highlighted with gold.

The elegant effect of many English and American wallpapers made during the late 19th century was produced by embossing. Because of the expense involved, few reproductions of embossed papers are seen on the market today. One type that is available, however, is called Anaglypta. Anaglypta was one of the many imitations of an embossed, linoleumlike wallcovering called Lincrusta-Walton. Reproduction Anaglypta is available in white only; color can be applied once it is hung. Another type of textured (rather than embossed) wallpaper that was popular from the 1880s into the 1920s was ingrain or oatmeal paper. Oatmeal paper is considered an unsuitable wallcovering today because of its rough, unwashable surface.

By the 1890s designers had stopped emphasizing the use of wallpaper in "tasteful" interiors; wallpaper patterns lost their "designer look." Manufacturers returned to producing patterns with floral and scroll motifs, rendered in a much less stylized manner. A small interest in Art Nouveau patterns existed; however, Art Nouveau never evolved into a major wallpaper style. People looking for formal designs found papers reminiscent of late 18th-century neoclassical styles, such as "Large Adams" (page 86); the inspiration for the design, however, was 18th-century architectural decoration, not 18th-century wallpaper design.

Even as late as the early 1970s, few reproductions of Victorian papers were to be found. Today, the strong interest in late Victorian design is reflected in the market. No longer is red-flocked wallpaper (not available as a reproduction) the only paper that symbolizes a period rich in design.

WALLPAPERS

BRADBURY AND BRADBURY

In addition to reproductions of historic wallpapers, Bradbury and Bradbury offers adaptations of wallpapers and wall treatments derived from design books published in the late 19th century. Most Bradbury and Bradbury papers are available in four period colorways created according to late 19th-century color theory. Only document colors are listed. Bradbury and Bradbury papers are ordered by pattern name and color.

BRIAR ROSE. English, 1900–10, machine print. Oman and Hamilton, fig. 1242, p. 443. 27″ wide, 9″ repeat, 5 yds. per s/r. Adaptation of a design by C.F.A. Vosey. Document at Victoria and Albert Museum.

CAMPBELL HOUSE DAMASK. American, 1870–90, machine print. 24″ wide, 12″ repeat, 5 yds. per s/r. Reproduced for Campbell House Foundation, St. Louis, Mo.

DRESSER ROOM SET. English, 1870–80. A set taken from designs of Christopher Dresser, including a dado paper, chair-rail border, fill paper, frieze and ceiling paper.

GRIFFIN. English, 1895–1900. 27″ wide, 13½″ repeat, 5 yds. per s/r. Adaptation of a published design by Lewis F. Day.

LILY. American, 1875–80. 21″ wide plus 4″ border, 10½″ repeat, 5

PLAZA HOTEL
WALLPAPER AND
BORDER, 1880–1900.
Bradbury and Bradbury.
Burnt orange and cream.

CAMPBELL HOUSE
DAMASK, 1870–90.
Bradbury and Bradbury.

MAREIKO, 1870–1900.
Brunschwig and Fils.
Aubergine.

yds. per s/r. Adaptation of a sketch for a wall treatment by P.B. Wight. Document at Burnham Architectural Library, Chicago.

❧ OGLESBY DAMASK. English or American, 1870–80, machine print. 22½" wide, 8¾" repeat, 28 sq. ft. per s/r. Reproduced for Governor Oglesby Mansion, Decatur, Ill. Red, brown and gold.

❧ PLAZA HOTEL WALLPAPER AND BORDER. American, 1880–1900, machine print. 18" wide plus 6" border, 12" repeat. Reproduced for Plaza Hotel Saloon, San Juan Bautista, Calif. Burnt orange and cream.

❧ SAVARIC. English, 1895, machine print. 27" wide, 13½" repeat, 5 yds. per s/r. 13% reduction in scale. Document at Victoria and Albert Museum.

❧ SWYRE CROSS. English, 1873, machine print. 27" wide, 25½" repeat, 5 yds. per s/r.

BRUNSCHWIG AND FILS

❧ FUCHSIA TRELLIS. French or English, 1870–85, block print. 18½" wide, 23" repeat, 7 yds. per s/r. Document at Cooper-Hewitt Museum. No. 12514.06 (pistachio).

❧ JAPANESQUE. American, 1870–90, machine print. 24½" wide, 15¾" half-drop repeat, 5 yds. per s/r. Ground color not reproduced exactly. Document at Cooper-Hewitt Museum. No. 12493.06 (gold on light brown).

❧ MAREIKO. French or English, 1870–1900, machine print. 27" wide, 23½" repeat, 5 yds. per s/r. Increased width and addition of similar motif. Document at Cooper-Hewitt Museum. No. 12487.06 (aubergine).

CAMRON-STANFORD HOUSE PRESERVATION ASSOCIATION

❧ HEWES PARLOR PAPER. English, 1875–85, machine print. Lynn, color plate 89, p. 352, and dust jacket. 21" wide, 19" repeat, 5 yds. per s/r. Document at Cooper-Hewitt Museum. Special order.

COLE AND SON

Most of the designs listed are available as special orders. Custom color can be printed.

❧ ACANTHUS. English, 1870–90, machine print. 21" wide, 46" repeat, 11 yds. per s/r. No. 98874 (red).

❧ AUDLEY END. English, 1890–1900, machine print. 21" wide, 17" repeat, 11 yds. per s/r. No. 98870 (terra cotta).

❧ BEATRIX DESIGN. English, 1880–90, machine print. 21" wide, 21" repeat, 11 yds. per s/r. Adaptation. No. OEW143 (tan). Alternate color: No. OEW144 (brown).

❧ CELTIC. English, 1890, machine print. 21" wide, 8" repeat, 11 yds. per s/r. No. 98885 (blue on green). Alternate color: No. 98886 (brown on gold).

❧ LARGE ADAMS. English, 1890–1900, machine print. 21" wide, 24" repeat, 11 yds. per s/r. No. 98816 (white on blue).

top left
ACANTHUS, 1870–90.
Cole and Son. Red.

top right
HEWES PARLOR PAPER,
1875–85. Camron-
Stanford House.

right
LARGE ADAMS,
1890–1900. Cole and Son.
White on blue.

FUCHSIA TRELLIS,
1870–85. Brunschwig and
Fils. Pistachio.

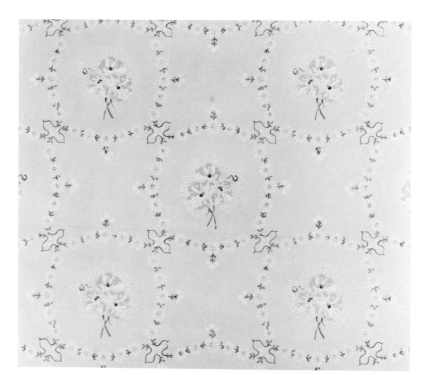

BARTON HOUSE RES-
TORATION BEDROOM,
1900. Scalamandré. Pink
and green on white.

BARTON LILY, 1900.
Scalamandré. Pink and
green on brown.

POPPY. English, 1880–1900, machine print. 21″wide, 17″repeat, 11 yds. per s/r. No. 98887 (pink and brown).

ROYSTON. English, 1890–1900, machine print. 21″ wide, 28″ repeat, 11 yds. per s/r. No. PR15013 (green ground).

COWTAN AND TOUT

ADAM AND BORDER. English or American, 1890–1900, machine print. 22″ wide plus 5″ border, 22″ repeat, 5 yds. per s/r. No. 13691-6 (bright yellow).*

MARLBOROUGH STRIPE. English or American, 1880–1900, machine print. 21″ wide, 5½ yds. per s/r. No. 29072 (beige). Alternate color: No. 29071 (red).*

PILLEMENT. English or American, 1890–1910, machine print. 24″ wide, 27″ repeat, 5 yds. per s/r. No. 11015 (gray, white-green-white).*

WESTERN BIRDS. English, 1870–90, block print. 21″ wide, 20″ repeat. No. 27120 (multi on white).*

WINDSOR ROSE. English or American, 1890–1900, machine print. 27″ wide, 36″ repeat, 5 yds. per s/r. Adaptation. No. 82000 (multi on beige).*

LEE JOFA

RIBBON AND TRAIL TRELLIS. American or English, 1880–1900, machine print. 27″ wide, 15⅝″ repeat, 5 yds. per s/r. No. P779003 (cream).*

SCALAMANDRÉ

ACORN HALL DINING ROOM. American, 1890–1900, machine print. 28″wide, 18¾″repeat, 5 yds. per s/r. Reproduced for Acorn Hall, Morristown, N.J. No. WP81068-1 (red and white on metallic ground). Special order.

ACORN HALL LIBRARY. English or American, 1870–90, machine print. 24″ wide, 12″ repeat. Reproduced for Acorn Hall, Morristown, N.J. No. WP81067-1 (gold on burgundy fabric).

BARTON HOUSE RESTORATION. American, 1890–1900, machine print. 36⅜″ wide, 22″ repeat, 4 yds. per s/r. Reproduced for Barton House, Lubbock, Tex. No. WP81116-1 (beige and gold).

BARTON HOUSE RESTORATION. American, 1890–1910, machine print. 27″wide, 26″repeat. Adaptation. Reproduced for Barton House, Lubbock, Tex. No. WP81126-1 (red and green on metallic ground).

BARTON HOUSE RESTORATION BEDROOM. American, c. 1900, machine print. 27″ wide, 15½″ repeat. Reproduced for Barton House, Lubbock, Tex. No. WP81110-1 (pink and green on white).

BARTON HOUSE RESTORATION HALL WALLS. American, c. 1900, machine print. 46¾″ wide, 18¾″ repeat, 3 yds. per s/r. Reproduced for Barton House. No. WP81105-1 (beige and brown).

FAIRFIELD PLANTA-
TION PAPER, 1870–80.
Scalamandré. Beige
on gray.

MONTEZUMA
GEOMETRIC, 1890–1900.
Scalamandré. Copper and
tan on green.

୧ BARTON LILY. American, c. 1900, machine print. 45″ wide, 22″ repeat, 3 yds. per s/r. Reproduced for Barton House, Lubbock, Tex. No. WP81115-1 (pink and green on brown).

୧ FAIRFIELD PLANTATION PAPER. English or American, 1870–80, machine print. 27″ wide, 18″ repeat, 5 yds. per s/r. Historic Charleston Reproductions. No.WP81273-1 (beige on gray).

୧ HIRSCHFELD HOUSE DOWNSTAIRS MAIN HALL. American, 1890–1910, machine print. 18″ wide, 19″ repeat, 8 yds. per s/r. Reproduced for Hirschfeld House, Austin, Tex. No.WP81192-1 (maroon and brown on beige).

୧ LAWNFIELD. American, 1890–1910, machine print. 18″ wide, 19″ repeat, 8 yds. per s/r. Reproduced for Lawnfield, Mentor, Ohio. No. WP81187-1 (multi on ivory).

୧ THE MOLLY BROWN HOUSE. American, 1890–1900, machine print. 18⅝″ wide, 18¾″ repeat, 8 yds. per s/r. Reproduced for Molly Brown House, Denver, Colo. No.WP81229-1 (black and red on ecru).

୧ MONTEZUMA FLORAL. American, 1890–1900, machine print. 36″ wide, 18¾″ repeat, 4 yds. per s/r. Document at Villa Montezuma, San Diego, Calif. No.WP81132-1 (multi on bronze).

୧ MONTEZUMA GEOMETRIC. American. 1890–1900, machine print. 27″ wide, 6½″ repeat, 5 yds. per s/r. Document at Villa Montezuma, San Diego, Calif. No.WP81128-1 (copper and tan on green).

୧ NATHANIEL ORR HOUSE PARLOR. American, 1890–1900, machine print. 18″ wide, 18⁹⁄₁₆″ repeat, 8 yds. per s/r. Reproduced for Steilacoom Historical Museum, Steilacoom, Wash. No. WP81243-1 (mottled).

୧ ORIENTAL DIVERSION. American, 1890–1900, machine print. 48″ wide, 15⅝″ repeat. No.WP81058-5 (green ground).*

୧ PETERSON HOUSE. American, 1880–1900, machine print. 20″ wide, 8¼″ repeat, 7 yds. per s/r. Reconstructed from photograph. No. WP81181-1 (white and tan).

୧ PHOENIX TILE. American, 1890–1900, machine print. 27″ wide, 6″ repeat, 5 yds. per s/r. Reproduced for Rosson House, Phoenix, Ariz. No.WP81152-1 (blue and white).

୧ PHOENIX WALLS. American, c. 1900, machine print. 20½″ wide, 22½″ repeat, 7 yds. per s/r. Reproduced for Rosson House, Phoenix, Ariz. No.WP81150-1 (multi on brown).

୧ ROSSON DINING ROOM. American, 1880–90, machine print. 36″ wide, 15½″ repeat, 4 yds. per s/r. Reproduced for Rosson House, Phoenix, Ariz. No.WP81151-1 (gray and gold on brown).

୧ ROSSON NURSERY. American, 1890–1900, machine print. 24⅛″ wide, 15½″ repeat, 6 yds. per s/r. Reproduced for Rosson House, Phoenix, Ariz. No.WP81185-1 (pink and blue on beige).

୧ ROSSON TILE. American, 1890–1900, machine print. 25″ wide, 6⅛″ repeat, 6 yds. per s/r. Reproduced for Rosson House, Phoenix, Ariz. No.WP81155-1 (blue on white).

ROSSON DINING
ROOM, 1880–90.
Scalamandré. Gray and
gold on brown.

THOMAS WOLFE
MEMORIAL DINING
ROOM, 1880–1900.
Scalamandré. Red ground.

🖝 ROSSON WALLS. American, c. 1900, machine print. 48″ wide, 7¾″ repeat, 3 yds. per s/r. Reproduced for Rosson House, Phoenix, Ariz. No. WP81163-1 (pink and peach).

🖝 SAGAMORE HILL LIBRARY FIELD PAPER. English, 1880–1900, machine embossed. 18³⁄₁₆″ wide, 15¾″ repeat, 8 yds. per s/r. Reproduced for Sagamore Hill, Oyster Bay, N.Y. No. WP81259-1 (gold textured). Special order.

🖝 SAVANNAH TULIP. American, c. 1900, machine print. 27″ wide, 18½″ repeat. Savannah Collection. Document at 419 East Congress Street, Savannah, Ga. No. WP81092-1 (brown on bisque).

🖝 SCHREINER ROSE. American, 1880–1900, roller print. 19″ wide, 19″ repeat, 8 yds. per s/r. Reproduced for Schreiner Mansion, Kerrville, Tex. No. WP81235-1 (rose on green ground).

🖝 SCHREINER STRIPE. American, 1880–1900, machine print. 18″ wide, 15³⁄₈″ repeat, 8 yds. per s/r. Reproduced for Schreiner Mansion, Kerrville, Tex. No. WP81244-1 (tan). Special order.

THOMAS WOLFE
MEMORIAL HALL
WALLS, 1880–1900.
Scalamandré. Silver,
green and beige.

&❧ SORRELL-WEED HOUSE. Probably American, 1870–90, machine print. 48″ wide, 22½″ repeat, 3 yds. per s/r. Savannah Collection. Document at Sorrell-Weed House, Savannah, Ga. No. WP81119-1 (celadon and white).

&❧ TELLER'S THISTLE. American, c. 1900, machine print. 48″ wide, 20″ repeat, 3 yds. per s/r. Central City Collection. No. WP81145-1 (birch color ground).

&❧ THOMAS WOLFE MEMORIAL DINING ROOM. American, 1880–1900, machine print. 24½″ wide, 7¹⁵⁄₁₆″ repeat, 6 yds. per s/r. Reproduced for Thomas Wolfe Memorial, Asheville, N.C. No. WP81197-1 (red ground).

&❧ THOMAS WOLFE MEMORIAL HALL WALLS. American, 1880–1900, machine print. 24½″ wide, 7¹⁵⁄₁₆″ repeat, 6 yds. per s/r. Reproduced for Thomas Wolfe Memorial, Asheville, N.C. No. WP81198-1 (silver, green and beige).

SCHUMACHER

❧ BERESFORD FILLER. English, 1870–80, machine print. 20½″ wide, 15⅝″ repeat, 7 yds. per s/r. Document at Victoria and Albert Museum. No. 3852A (document brown). Alternate colors: No. 3852C (azure); No. 3852D (celadon); No. 3852E (beige).

❧ BILTMORE DAMASK. English or American, 1910, machine print. 20½″ wide, 12⅝″ repeat, 7 yds. per s/r. Document at Biltmore House, Asheville, N.C. No. 3850A (document linen).

❧ BILTMORE FLOCK. English or American, 1890–1910, machine print with flocking. 20½″ wide, 4″ repeat, 7 yds. per s/r. Adaptation. Document at Biltmore House, Asheville, N.C. No. 3846A (document beige).

❧ BILTMORE FOLIATE. American or English, 1900–10, machine print. 20½″ wide, 20½″ repeat, 7 yds. per s/r. Document at Biltmore House, Asheville, N.C. No. 3844A (document pewter). Alternate color: No. 3844 series.

❧ JAPANESQUE. American, 1880–1900, machine print. 20½″ wide, 19″ repeat, 7 yds. per s/r. Document at Cooper-Hewitt Museum. No. 3815A (document blue). Alternate color: No. 3851D (taupe).

RICHARD E. THIBAUT

❧ ALLEN ROSE. American, 1880–1900, machine print. 28″ wide, 22″ repeat, 5 yds. per s/r. Number of colors reduced from 16 to 10; width of pattern increased. Reproduced for Historic House Association of America. Document at Candace Allen House, Providence, R.I. No. 839-T-6523 (multi on white).

❧ JONESBORO. American, 1880–90, machine print. 28″ wide, 16″ repeat, 5 yds. per s/r. Reproduced for Historic House Association of America. Document at Deaderick-Wilster House, Jonesboro, Tenn. No. 839-T-6591 (green ground).

❧ KIRKWOOD SQUARE. American, 1880–1900, machine print. 28″ wide, 11″ repeat, 5 yds. per s/r. Reproduced for Historic House Association of America. Document at Kirkwood, Eutaw, Ala. No. 839-T-6583 (black on green ground).

❧ WALLA WALLA STRIPE. American, 1880–1900, machine print. 28″ wide, 16″ repeat, 5 yds. per s/r. Reproduced for Historic House Association of America. Document at Kirkman House, Walla Walla, Wash. No. 839-T-6518 (red).

❧ WALNUT ROOM. English, 1890–1910, block print. 28″ wide, 25¼″ repeat, 5 yds. per s/r. Width increased by 7″. Reproduced for Historic House Association of America. Document at Biltmore, Asheville, N.C. No. 839-T-6569 (off-white ground).

WATERHOUSE WALLHANGINGS

❧ BRODSWORTH. English or American, 1880–1900, machine print. 27″ wide, 30″ repeat, 5 yds. per s/r. Document in Waterhouse Archives. No. 187540 (red).

KIRKWOOD SQUARE, 1880–1900. Richard E. Thibaut. Black on green ground.

BRODSWORTH, 1880–1900. Waterhouse Wallhangings. Red.

WALNUT ROOM, 1890–
1910. Richard E. Thibaut.
Off-white ground.

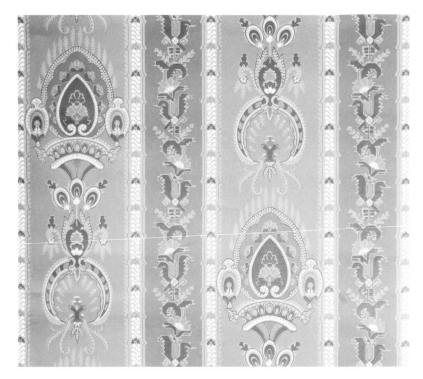

WALLA WALLA STRIPE,
1880–1900. Richard E.
Thibaut. Red.

ALLEN ROSE, 1880–1900.
Richard E. Thibaut. Multi
on white.

EASTLAKE FRIEZE,
1870—80. Bradbury and
Bradbury. Blue and gold.

ᔰ CHINESE POPPY. English, 1870–80, machine print. 18½″ wide, 18½″ repeat, 7 yds. per s/r. Document in Waterhouse Archives. No. 146467 (red on beige).

ᔰ GEORGETOWN FLORAL. American, c. 1900, machine print. 20½″ wide, 19″ repeat, 7yds. per s/r. Document in Waterhouse Archives. No. 192519 (gray-green ground).

ᔰ PILLEMENT. French, late 19th century, block print. 28″ wide, 44″ repeat, 5 yds. per s/r. Document in Waterhouse Archives. No. 100635 (multi on white).

ᔰ QUINCY LACE. English or American, 1890–1900, machine print. 20½″ wide, 18″ repeat, 7 yds. per s/r. Document in Waterhouse Archives. No. 180163 (yellow). Alternate colors: series.

ᔰ TOWNHOUSE STRIPE. Probably American, 1890–1910, machine print. 20½″ wide, 7 yds. per s/r. Document in Waterhouse Archives. Period colorings: No. 189518 (yellow and white); No. 189488 (beige and white); No. 189484 (light and dark blue); No. 189635 (brown and white); No. 189613 (gray and white).

ᔰ VASSALL ADAMS HOUSE. Probably American, 1870–1900, machine print. 26½″ wide, 18″ repeat, 5 yds. per s/r. Reproduced for Adams National Historic Site, Quincy, Mass. No. 171575 (rust ground).

ᔰ WAYSIDE FLORAL. American, 1870–90, machine print. 25″ wide, 15¾″ repeat, 5 yds. per s/r. Document at The Wayside, Concord, Mass. No. 142635 (white on beige).

BRADBURY AND BRADBURY

BORDERS, DADOS AND PANELS

In addition to reproductions of historic wallpapers, Bradbury and Bradbury offers adaptations of wallpapers and wall treatments derived from design books published in the late 19th century. Most Bradbury and Bradbury papers are available in four period colorways created according to late 19th-century color theory. Only document colors are listed. Bradbury and Bradbury papers are ordered by pattern name and color.

ᔰ DEER AND RABBIT FRIEZE. English, 1887, block print. 18″ with 5½″ related border, 19″ repeat. Minor changes in design. Document at Victoria and Albert Museum.

ᔰ EASTLAKE DADO. English or American, 1870–80, machine print. 22″ wide, 3″ repeat, 5 yds. per s/r. Adaptation. Reproduced for Camron-Stanford House, Oakland, Calif. Blue and gold.

ᔰ EASTLAKE FRIEZE. English or American, 1870–80, machine print. Greysmith, fig. 105, p. 146; Lynn, color plate 92, p. 435. 18″ plus borders, 12″ repeat. Adaptation. Reproduced for Camron-Stanford House, Oakland, Calif. Document at Cooper-Hewitt Museum. Blue and gold.

ᔰ PEACOCK FRIEZE. English, 1889. 21¾″ wide, 21¾″ repeat. Adapted from a wallpaper advertisement design by Walter Crane. Document at the Victoria and Albert Museum.

ᔰ PERSIA BORDERS. French, 1870–80, machine print. 10″ wide, 18″ repeat. Adapted from a design by Racinet.

BERESFORD BORDER, 1870–80. Schumacher. Document brown.

&❧ VERMILLION STAR FRIEZE. English or American, 1890–1900, machine print. 18″ wide, 9½″ repeat. Reproduced from photograph. Reproduced for Clay County Historical Society, Vermillion, S.D.

CAMRON-STANFORD HOUSE PRESERVATION ASSOCIATION

&❧ HEWES PARLOR BORDER. English, 1875–85, machine print. Lynn, color plate 89, p. 352; dust jacket. 21″ wide, 5″ repeat. Document at Cooper-Hewitt Museum. Special order.

SCALAMANDRÉ

&❧ BARTON HOUSE RESTORATION HALL CHAIR RAIL. American, c. 1900, machine print. 47½″ wide, 18¾″ repeat, 3 yds. per s/r. Reproduced for Barton House, Lubbock, Tex. No.WP81104-1 (brown).

&❧ CATALDO MISSION BORDER. English or American, 1870–1900, machine print. 4⅞″ wide, 18¼″ repeat. Reproduced for Old Mission, Cataldo, Idaho. No.BD 600-1 (rose and terra cotta).

&❧ MONTEZUMA DADO. English or American, 1890–1900, machine print. 36″ wide, 20⅝″ repeat. Reproduced for Villa Montezuma, San Diego, Calif. No.WP81131-1 (multi).

&❧ MONTEZUMA FLORAL BORDER. American, 1890–1900, machine print. 8″ wide, 15¹¹⁄₁₆″ repeat. Reproduced for Villa Montezuma, San Diego, Calif. No.WPBD81130-1 (multi on bronze).

&❧ PHOENIX FRIEZE. American, c. 1900, machine print. 18″ wide, 22⅛″ repeat. Reproduced for Rosson House, Phoenix, Ariz. No. WPBD81161-1 (multi on brown).

ROSE SWAG BORDER. American, 1890–1900, machine print. 18″ wide, 14″ repeat. Adaptation. Central City Collection. No. WPBD 81142-1 (green and pink on yellow).

ROSSON HOUSE FRIEZE. American, c. 1900, machine print. 17″ wide, 9⅜″ repeat. Reproduced for Rosson House, Phoenix, Ariz. No. WPBD81147-1 (pink).

SAGAMORE HILL LIBRARY FRIEZE. English or American, 1880–1900, machine print. 9½″ wide, 18³⁄₁₆″ repeat. Design reconstructed from photographs. Reproduced for Sagamore Hill, Oyster Bay, N.Y. No.WP81258 (bronze and green). Special order.

SAVANNAH HOUSE BORDER. American, 1890–1900, machine print. 18½″ wide, 19″ repeat. Savannah Collection. Document at Werms House, Savannah, Ga. No.WPBD81087-1 (brown and rust on beige).

STANROD PANEL. American, c. 1900, machine print. 27″ wide, 8′ panel, 2 panels per s/r. Reproduced for Stanrod, Pocatello, Idaho. No. WP81073-1 (green on white).

SCHUMACHER

BERESFORD BORDER. English, 1870–80, machine print. 4⅝″wide, 16″ repeat. Document at Victoria and Albert Museum. No. 5700A (document brown). Alternate colors: No. 5700C (azure); No. 5700D (persimmon); No.5700E (dusty rose).

BERESFORD CORNICE. English, 1870–80, machine print. 8¼″ wide, 20½″ repeat. Document at Victoria and Albert Museum. No.

BERESFORD CORNICE, 1870–80. Schumacher. Document brown.

BERESFORD DADO,
1870–80. Schumacher.
Document brown.

CHRYSANTHEMUM
BORDER, 1890–1900.
Schumacher. Document
blue and yellow.

PLAZA HOTEL CEILING,
1880–1900. Bradbury and
Bradbury. Gold on gray.

5701A (document brown). Alternate colors: No. 5701C (azure); No. 5701D (persimmon); No. 5701E (dusty rose).

&❧ BERESFORD DADO. English, 1870–80, machine print. 20½″wide, 6¾″ repeat, 7 yds. per s/r. Document at Victoria and Albert Museum. No. 3853A (document brown). Alternate colors: No. 3853C (azure); No. 3853D (celadon); No. 3853E (beige).

&❧ CHRYSANTHEMUM BORDER. English or American, 1890–1900, machine print. 9″wide, 10″repeat. Document at Whitworth Art Gallery, Manchester, England. No. 5702A (document blue and yellow).

RICHARD E. THIBAUT

&❧ BACHELOR'S PEAR VINE. English or American, 1880–1900, machine print. 28″wide, 12½″repeat, 5 yds. per s/r. Reproduced for Historic House Association of America. Document at Hanger House, Little Rock, Ark. No. 839-T-6546 (orange and gold on beige).

&❧ JONESBORO BORDER. American, 1880–90, machine print. 6″ wide, 15¾″ repeat. Reproduced for Historic House Association of America. Document at Deaderick-Wilster House, Jonesboro, Tenn. No. 839-T-650091 (green ground).

CEILING PAPERS

BRADBURY AND BRADBURY

In addition to reproductions of historic wallpapers, Bradbury and Bradbury offers adaptations of wallpapers and wall treatments derived from design books published in the late 19th century. Most Bradbury and Bradbury papers are available in four period colorways created according to late 19th-century color theory. Only document colors are listed. Bradbury and Bradbury papers are ordered by pattern name and color.

&❧ PLAZA HOTEL CEILING. American, 1880–1900, machine print. 27″wide, 9″repeat, 5 yds. per s/r. Reproduced for Plaza Hotel Saloon, San Juan Bautista, Calif. Gold on gray.

&❧ RANDOM STAR CEILING. English, 1870–90. 27″wide, 27″repeat, 5 yds. per s/r. Adapted from design of Christopher Dresser.

SCALAMANDRÉ

&❧ BARTON HOUSE RESTORATION BEDROOM CEILING. American, c. 1900, machine print. 48″wide, 12½″repeat, 3 yds. per s/r. Reproduced for Barton House, Lubbock, Tex. No.WP81136-1 (pink and green on white).

&❧ BARTON HOUSE RESTORATION HALL CEILING. American, 1890–1900, machine print. 48″wide, 1½″repeat, 3 yds. per s/r. Reproduced for Barton House, Lubbock, Tex. No. WP81101-1 (beige and gold).

&❧ HIRSHFELD HOUSE DOWNSTAIRS MAIN HALL CEILING. American, 1890–1900, machine print. 20″wide, 6″repeat, 7 yds. per s/r. Reproduced for Hirshfeld House, Austin, Tex. No. WP81193-1 (metallic on beige).

BACHELOR'S PEAR
VINE, 1880–1900.
Richard E. Thibaut.
Orange and gold on beige.

SALUBRA TEKKO,
1890–1910. Scalamandré.

HANGER HOUSE
GARDEN, 1880–90.
Richard E. Thibaut. Pink
and green on beige.

HANGER HOUSE,
1880–90. Richard E.
Thibaut. Burgundy
and gold.

MONTEZUMA CEILING,
1890–1900. Scalamandré.
Green and metallic on
terra cotta.

❧ HIRSHFELD HOUSE UPSTAIRS HALL CEILING. American, 1890–1900, machine print. 20″wide, 24″repeat, 7 yds. per s/r. Reproduced for Hirshfeld House, Austin, Tex. No. WP81194-1 (copper on tan).

❧ MONTEZUMA CEILING. American, 1890–1900, machine print. 35½″ wide, 15¹³/₁₆″ repeat, 4 yds. per s/r. Document at Villa Montezuma, San Diego, Calif. No. WP81127-1 (green and metallic on terra cotta).

❧ THOMAS WOLFE MEMORIAL HALL CEILING. American, 1880–1900, machine print. 27″wide, 5⅝″repeat, 5 yds. per s/r. Reproduced for Thomas Wolfe Memorial, Asheville, N.C. No. WP81199-1 (brown on gray).

❧ WERMS HOUSE FRIEZE. American, 1870–80, machine print. 48″wide, 6″repeat, 3 yds. per s/r. Adaptation. Savannah Collection. Document at Werms House, Savannah, Ga. No. WP81112-1 (green and ecru on beige).

RICHARD E. THIBAUT

❧ HANGER HOUSE. English or American, 1880–1900, machine print. 28″wide, 22″repeat, 5 yds. per s/r. Pattern reconstructed from photograph. Reproduced for Historic House Association of America. Document at Hanger House, Little Rock, Ark. No. 839-T-6544 (burgundy and gold).

❧ HANGER HOUSE GARDEN. English or American, 1880–1900, machine print. 28″wide, 20½″repeat, 5 yds. per s/r. Pattern reconstructed from photograph. Reproduced for Historic House Association of America. Document at Hanger House, Little Rock, Ark. No. 839-T-6545 (pink and green on beige).

OATMEAL PAPERS

CLARENCE HOUSE

The composition of period oatmeal or ingrain wallpapers is not suitable for a modern wallpaper product. Papers that simulate this effect through printing are available from Clarence House, Special Effects Collection, 21″wide: No. C906 (wet sand); No. C962 (clay); No. C986 (camel); No. C1046 (pale sepia).

EMBOSSED PAPERS

SCALAMANDRÉ

❧ SALUBRA TEKKO. Austria (now produced in Switzerland), 1890–1900, machine embossed. 31½″ wide, 10¼″ repeat, 5 yds. per s/r. No. 36-524 (blue).*

❧ SALUBRA TEKKO. Austria (now produced in Switzerland), 1890–1900, machine embossed. 31½″ wide, 22″ repeat, 5 yds. per s/r. No. 38-535 (gold).*

❧ SALUBRA TEKKO. Austria (now produced in Switzerland), 1890–1910, machine embossed. 31½″ wide, 20½″ repeat, 5 yds. per s/r. No. 42-504 (green gold).*

ᶓ◗ SALUBRA TEKKO. Austria (now produced in Switzerland), 1890–1900, machine embossed. 31½″ wide, 2¼″ repeat, 5 yds. per s/r. No. 43-573 (gold).*

ANAGLYPTA

BRUNSCHWIG AND FILS

ᶓ◗ COLUMBINE. English, 1880–1910, machine embossed. 21″ wide, 4″ repeat, 11 yds. per s/r. Document in Brunschwig Archives. No. 10470.06 (white).

SAN FRANCISCO VICTORIANA

In addition to the reproduction Anaglypta listed, San Francisco Victoriana carries eight antique embossed borders. They range in width from 3″ to 14½″ and were made in Germany between 1890 and 1915.

ᶓ◗ ACANTHUS. English, 1880–1910, machine embossed. 20½″ wide, 10½″ repeat, 11 yds. per s/r. No. 314 (white).

ᶓ◗ ANITA. English, 1880–1910, machine embossed. 21″ wide, 3⅛″ repeat, 11 yds. per s/r. No. 328 (white).

ᶓ◗ APEX. English, 1880–1900, machine embossed. 21″ wide, 10½″ repeat, 11 yds. per s/r. No. 303 (white).

ᶓ◗ BEAUFORT. English, 1880–1910, machine embossed. 20½″ wide, 10½″ repeat, 11 yds. per s/r. No. 630 (white; super heavy).

ᶓ◗ CALIOPE. English, 1880–1910, machine embossed. 20⅜″ wide, 5¼″ repeat, 11 yds. per s/r. No. 315 (white).

ᶓ◗ CANDIA. English, 1880–1910, machine embossed. 20½″ wide, 2⅝″ repeat, 11 yds. per s/r. No. 325 (white).

ᶓ◗ CELESTINE. English, 1880–1910, machine embossed. 21″ wide, 5¼″ repeat, 11 yds. per s/r. No. 125 (white).

ᶓ◗ FLORELLA. English, 1880–1910, machine embossed. 20½″ wide, 1¼″ repeat, 11 yds. per s/r. No. 312 (white).

ᶓ◗ INTRIGUE. English, 1880–1910, machine embossed. 21″ wide, 10½″ repeat, 11 yds. per s/r. No. 300 (white).

ᶓ◗ KENILWORTH. English, 1880–1910, machine embossed. 21″ wide, 10½″ repeat, 11 yds. per s/r. No. 199 (white).

ᶓ◗ MADELEINE. English, 1880–1910, machine embossed. 21″ wide, 7″ repeat, 11 yds. per s/r. No. 193 (white).

ᶓ◗ PETAL. English, 1880–1910, machine embossed. 20⅝″ wide, 10½″ repeat, 11 yds. per s/r. No. 636 (white; super heavy).

ᶓ◗ REGENCY. English, 1880–1910, machine embossed. 20⅞″ wide, 1¾″ repeat, 11 yds. per s/r. No. 181 (white).

SCHUMACHER

ᶓ◗ ANAGLYPTA DAMASK. English or American, 1880–1910, machine embossed. 21″ wide, 21″ repeat, 5½ yds. per s/r. No. 181-2 (white).

ᶓ◗ ANAGLYPTA HIGH RELIEF. English or American, 1880–1910, machine embossed. 21″ wide, 5¼″ repeat, 5½ yds. per s/r. No. 181-1 (white).

MARIGOLD, 1875. Brad-
bury and Bradbury.

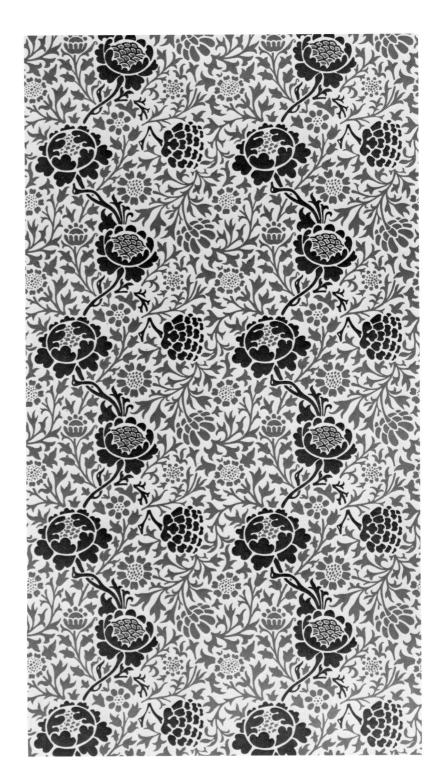

GRAFTON, 1883. Bradbury and Bradbury.

❧ ANAGLYPTA STAMPED CEILING. English or American, 1880–1910, machine embossed. 21″wide, 7″repeat, 5½ yds. per s/r. No. 181-3 (white).

A.L. DIAMENT AND COMPANY

SCENIC PAPERS

❧ APPIAN WAY. French, 1900–30, block print. 7′ 8½″ per set, 18½″ per strip, 5 strips per set. No. 20066-007 (gray).

❧ CAMPAGNE. French, 1900–30, block print. 13′ 10½″ per set, 18½″ per strip, 9 strips per set. No. 20069-007 (gray).

❧ COAST OF VILLEFRANCHE. French, 1900–30, block print. 21′ 7″ per set, 18½″ per strip, 14 strips per set. No. 20023-007 (multi on gray).

❧ ITALIAN LANDSCAPE. French, 1900–12, block print. 15′ per set, 18″ per strip, 10 strips per set. No. 20013-007 (gray background).

❧ ROMAN SPRING—FOUNTAIN OF VAUCLUSE. French, 1900–30, block print. 10′ 9½″ per set, 18½″ per strip, 7 strips per set. No. 20068-007 (multi).

❧ THE RUINS — PORT OF GOATS. French, 1900–30, block print. 10′ 9½″ per set, 18½″ per strip, 7 strips per set. No. 20067-007 (gray).

BRADBURY AND BRADBURY

WILLIAM MORRIS–STYLE PAPERS

In addition to reproductions of historic wallpapers, Bradbury and Bradbury offers adaptations of wallpapers and wall treatments derived from design books published in the late 19th century. Most Bradbury and Bradbury papers are available in four period colorways created according to late 19th-century color theory. Only document colors are listed. Bradbury and Bradbury papers are ordered by pattern name and color.

❧ APPLE. English, 1877, block print. Oman and Hamilton, fig. 1065, p. 372. 27″ wide, 10″ repeat, 5 yds. per s/r. 13% reduction in scale. Document at Victoria and Albert Museum.

❧ BALMORAL. English, 1887, block print. Oman and Hamilton, fig. 1073, p. 383. 27″ wide, 11″ repeat, 5 yds. per s/r. 13% reduction in scale. Document at Victoria and Albert Museum.

❧ BIRD AND ANEMONE. English, 1882, block print. Oman and Hamilton, fig. 1065, p. 377. 27″ wide, 22″ repeat, 5 yds. per s/r. 13% reduction in scale. Document at Victoria and Albert Museum.

❧ GRAFTON. English, 1883, block print. Oman and Hamilton, fig. 1065, p. 374. 27″ wide, 9″ repeat, 5 yds. per s/r. 13% reduction in scale. Document at Victoria and Albert Museum.

❧ MARIGOLD. English, 1875, block print. Lynn, fig. 16-5, p. 371. 27″ wide, 9″ repeat, 5 yds. per s/r. 13% reduction in scale. Document at Victoria and Albert Museum.

❧ MORRIS CEILING. English, 1888–89, block print. Oman and Hamilton, fig. 1065, p. 375. 27″ wide, 13½″ repeat, 5 yds. per s/r. 13% reduction in scale. Document at Victoria and Albert Museum.

❧ POPPY. English, 1881, block print. Oman and Hamilton, fig. 1065, p. 373. 27″ wide, 14″ repeat, 5 yds. per s/r. 13% reduction in scale. Document at Victoria and Albert Museum.

MORRIS CEILING, 1876.
Scalamandré. Multi greens.

WILLOW, 1874. Bradbury
and Bradbury.

MORRIS IRIS,
1887. Scalamandré.
Multi greens.

MYRTLE, 1899.
Scalamandré. Multi greens.

❧ WILLOW. English, 1874, block print. Oman and Hamilton, fig. 1065, p. 372; Lynn, fig. 16-6, p. 372. 27″ wide, 27″ repeat, 5 yds. per s/r. Adaptation. Document at Victoria and Albert Museum.

COLE AND SON
❧ HONEYSUCKLE. English, 1870–80, machine print. 21″ wide, 14″ repeat, 11 yds. per s/r. No. PR15043 (white on gray). Special order. Custom color can be printed.

COWTAN AND TOUT
❧ CANTERBURY BELLS. English, 1873, block print. Oman and Hamilton, fig. 1065, p. 372. 21″ wide, 12″ repeat, 5½ yds. per s/r. Color not reproduced exactly. "Lily" pattern by Morris. No. 25360-15 (multi green underprint).
❧ MICHAELMAS DAISY. English, 1880–90, block print. Oman and Hamilton, fig. 1076, p. 385. 21″ wide, 21″ repeat, 5 yds. per s/r. Adaptation. No. 25542 (orange and medium green).
❧ WILLOW LEAVES. English, 1870–90, block print. 24″ wide, 20″ repeat, 5 yds. per s/r. Adaptation. No. 25084 (beige and tan/cream).

SCALAMANDRÉ
❧ BORAGE. English, 1888–89, block print. Oman and Hamilton, fig. 1065, p. 375. 20⅞″ wide, 20⅞″ repeat, 7 yds. per s/r. Document at Victoria and Albert Museum. No. WP81240-1 (pearlized white).
❧ MORRIS CEILING. English, 1876, block print. Oman and Hamilton, fig. 1065, p. 374. 21″ wide, 21″ repeat, 7 yds. per s/r. "The Wreath" pattern by Morris. Document at Victoria and Albert Museum. No. WP81236-1 (multi greens).
❧ MORRIS IRIS. English, 1887, block print. Oman and Hamilton, fig. 1066, p. 377. 21″ wide, 17½″ repeat, 7 yds. per s/r. "Iris" pattern by Morris. Document at Victoria and Albert Museum. No. WP81239-1 (greens).
❧ MYRTLE. English, 1899, block print. 22¹⁄₁₆″ wide, 33¾″ repeat, 7 yds. per s/r. Document at Victoria and Albert Museum. No. WP81237-1 (multi greens).
❧ PIMPERNEL. English, 1876, block print. Oman and Hamilton, fig. 1065, p. 372; Greysmith, plate 22; Lynn, color plate 83, p. 346. 21¼″ wide, 16¹³⁄₁₆″ repeat, 7 yds. per s/r. Document at Victoria and Albert Museum. No. WP81226-1 (multi greens).
❧ WALLFLOWER. English, 1890, block print. Oman and Hamilton, fig. 1065, p. 375. 21″ wide, 14⁵⁄₁₆″ repeat, 7 yds. per s/r. Document at Victoria and Albert Museum. No. WP81233-1 (terra cotta).

APPENDIX

Many of the firms listed are wholesale houses whose products are available to the trade only. This means that their wallpapers are sold only through interior designers, architects and the decorating departments of fine retail and furniture stores. Some of these papers are also available through large wallpaper stores. In some cases, the firms will sell wallpapers directly to nonprofit institutions such as museums, historical societies, preservation organizations and state-owned historic properties; in other cases, they may refer interested persons to their local representative. Arrangements for custom reproductions should always be made through the manufacturer's main office.

LOUIS W. BOWEN. 979 Third Avenue, New York, N.Y. 10022

BRADBURY AND BRADBURY WALLPAPERS. P.O. Box 155, Benicia, Calif. 94510

BRUNSCHWIG AND FILS. 979 Third Avenue, New York, N.Y. 10022

THE CAMRON-STANFORD HOUSE PRESERVATION ASSOCIATION. 1418 Lakeside Drive, Oakland, Calif. 94612

CLARENCE HOUSE. 40 East 57th Street, New York, N.Y. 10022

COLE AND SON (WALLPAPERS) LTD. P.O. Box 4 BU, 18 Mortimer Street, London W1A 4BU, England (available in the United States exclusively through Clarence House)

COWTAN AND TOUT. 979 Third Avenue, New York, N.Y. 10022

A.L. DIAMENT AND COMPANY. P.O. Box 230, 309 Commerce Drive, Exton, Pa. 19341

GRACIE. 979 Third Avenue, New York, N.Y. 10022

PHILIP GRAF WALLPAPERS. 973 Third Avenue, New York, N.Y. 10022

KATZENBACH AND WARREN. 950 Third Avenue, New York, N.Y. 10022

LEE JOFA. 979 Third Avenue, New York, N.Y. 10022

SAN FRANCISCO VICTORIANA. 2245 Palow Avenue, San Francisco, Calif. 94124

SCALAMANDRÉ. 950 Third Avenue, New York, N.Y. 10022

SCHUMACHER. 939 Third Avenue, New York, N.Y. 10022

RICHARD E. THIBAUT. 315 Fifth Avenue, New York, N.Y. 10016

THE TWIGS. 5700 Third Avenue, San Francisco, Calif. 94124

ALBERT VAN LUIT AND COMPANY. 4000 Chevy Chase Drive, Los Angeles, Calif. 90039

WATERHOUSE WALLHANGINGS. 38 Wareham Street, Boston, Mass. 02118

WAVERLY FABRICS. 58 West 40th Street, New York, N.Y. 10018

ADAPTATION. A modern wallpaper that retains the overall appearance of the original document although certain changes have been made in the design. The term also may apply to a modern wallpaper produced as a companion to a reproduction fabric.

ANAGLYPTA. A patented uncolored wallpaper with a highly embossed design. The color is applied after the paper is hung.

BLOCK PRINTING. A process in which color is applied to paper by pressing a carved wooden block onto the paper.

COLORWAY. A manufacturer's term for identifying the predominant color or colors of a wallpaper design. Reproduction wallpapers are often available in several colorways. The document colorway copies the colors of the original wallpaper. The other colorways in which the reproduction design is available are created by the manufacturer to be compatible with modern decorating needs. Colorways that have a distinct period look are listed in this book as alternate colors.

DADO. The lower portion of the wall of a room, between the baseboard and the chair rail, often decorated differently from the upper section.

DOCUMENT. The original wallpaper whose design and color are copied for a reproduction wallpaper.

FLOCKING. A textured surface composed of chopped textile fibers glued to the paper.

GROUND. The background color of a wallpaper design.

INGRAIN PAPER. See oatmeal paper.

INTERPRETATION. A modern wallpaper in which one or more motifs from a document wallpaper are reworked into a new design.

MULTI. A manufacturer's term for a colorway containing many colors.

OATMEAL PAPER. A roughly textured paper made from pulp consisting of colored cotton or wool rags.

PAINTED PAPER. An 18th-century term for wallpaper.

PIECE. An 18th-century term for a roll of wallpaper.

PLAIN PAPER. A wallpaper decorated only with the ground color.

REPEAT. The dimension of one complete design element in a wallpaper.

REPRODUCTION WALLPAPER. A modern wallpaper that copies exactly the design, color and scale of an original wallpaper document.

ROLLER PRINTING. A process in which color is applied to a moving roll of paper by an engraved metal cylinder.

SANDWICH. Layers of wallpaper applied over a period of time. These are studied during historical research to determine the chronological sequence of application and the previous decorative styles of a historic building.

SCREEN PRINTING. A process, similar to stenciling, in which color is deposited on paper through a design cut into a fabric screen.

SIDEWALL. A modern term used to differentiate the wallpaper used on the wall from a border or dado paper; also called field or filler.

SELECTED
BIBLIOGRAPHY

This bibliography cites books and articles that are readily available and useful for an initial inquiry into the history and use of wallpapers. Both Oman and Hamilton's *Wallpapers* and Lynn's *Wallpapers in America* include extensive bibliographies. *Wallpapers in Historic Preservation* contains an excellent list of 19th-century publications that discuss contemporary attitudes towards wallpaper.

Clark, Fiona. *William Morris: Wallpapers and Chintzes.* London: Academy, 1973.

Clouzot, Henri, and Follot, Charles. *Histoire du Papier Peint en France.* Paris: Éditions D'Art Charles Moreau, 1935.

"Conservation of Historic Wallpaper," Special issue of the *Journal of the American Institute for Conservation of Historic and Artistic Works,* Spring 1981.

Cornforth, John. *English Interiors 1790–1848.* London: Barrie and Jenkins, 1978.

Dornsife, Samuel A. "Wallpaper." In *The Encyclopaedia of Victoriana,* edited by Harriet Bridgeman and Elizabeth Drury. New York: Macmillan, 1975.

Entwisle, Eric A. *The Book of Wallpaper.* London: Arthur Barker, 1954.

———. *French Scenic Wallpapers 1800–1860.* Leigh-on-Sea, England: F. Lewis, 1972.

———. *A Literary History of Wallpaper.* London: B.T. Batsford, 1960.

———. *Wallpapers of the Victorian Era.* Leigh-on-Sea, England: F. Lewis, 1964.

Fowler, John, and Cornforth, John. *English Decoration in the 18th Century.* Princeton, N.J.: Pyne Press, 1974.

Frangiamore, Catherine Lynn. *Wallpapers in Historic Preservation.* Washington, D.C.: National Park Service, U.S. Department of the Interior, 1977.

———. "Wallpaper: Technological Innovation and Changes in Design and Use." *Technological Innovation and the Decorative Arts: Winterthur Conference Report, 1973,* pp. 277–305. Charlottesville: University Press of Virginia, 1974.

———. "Wallpapers Used in Nineteenth Century America," *The Magazine Antiques,* December 1972, pp. 1042–51.

Greysmith, Brenda. *Wallpaper.* New York: Macmillan, 1976.

Hotchkiss, Horace. "Wallpaper Used in America, 1700–1850." In *The Concise Encyclopedia of American Antiques,* edited by Helen Comstock, vol. 2, pp. 488ff. New York: Hawthorne Books, 1958.

Lynn, Catherine. *Wallpaper in America from the Seventeenth Century to World War I.* New York: W.W. Norton, 1980.

Mayhew, Edgar de N., and Myers, Minor, Jr. *A Documentary History of American Interiors from the Colonial Era to 1915.* New York: Scribner's, 1980.

McClelland, Nancy V. *Historic Wall-Papers from Their Inception to the*

Introduction of Machinery. Philadelphia and London: J. B. Lippincott, 1924.

Musée des Arts Décoratifs. *Trois Siècles de Papiers Peints*. Paris: Musée des Arts Décoratifs, 1967.

Nouvel, Odile. *Wallpapers of France 1800–1850*. New York: Rizzoli, 1981.

Nylander, Richard C. "Elegant Late Nineteenth-Century Wallpapers," *The Magazine Antiques*, August 1982, pp. 284–87.

———. English Wallpaper in New England," *Country Life*, 26 April 1979, pp. 1304–07.

———. "Wallpaper and the Historic House." Slide tape. Nashville: American Association for State and Local History, 1977.

———. "Wallpaper Before 1830," *Early American Life*, February 1980, pp. 40–43.

Oman, Charles C. *Catalogue of Wallpapers, Victoria and Albert Museum*. London: 1929.

Oman, Charles C., and Hamilton, Jean. *Wallpapers: An International History and Illustrated Survey from the Victoria and Albert Museum*. New York: Abrams, 1982.

Peterson, Harold L. *Americans at Home*. New York: Scribner's, 1971. Reissued as *American Interiors: From Colonial Times to the Late Victorians*. New York: Scribner's, 1979.

Praz, Mario. *An Illustrated History of Furnishing from the Renaissance to the Twentieth Century*. New York: Braziller, 1964.

Sanborn, Kate. *Old Time Wall Papers*. Greenwich, Conn.: Literary Collector Press, 1905.

Seale, William. *Recreating the Historic House Interior*. Nashville: American Association for State and Local History, 1979.

———. *The Tasteful Interlude: American Interiors Through the Camera's Eye, 1860–1917*. New York: Praeger, 1975. Nashville: American Association for State and Local History, 1981.

Sugden, Alan V., and Edmondson, J. L. *A History of English Wallpaper, 1509–1914*. New York: Scribner's, 1925; London: B. T. Batsford, 1926.

Teynac, Françoise; Nolot, Pierre; and Vivian, Jean-Denis. *Wallpaper: A History*. New York: Rizzoli, 1982.

SOURCES OF
INFORMATION

AMERICAN SOCIETY OF INTERIOR DESIGNERS. 1430 Broadway, New York, N.Y. 10018

BOSCOBEL RESTORATION, INC. RFD 2, Garrison-on-Hudson, N.Y. 10524

COLONIAL WILLIAMSBURG FOUNDATION. P.O. Box C, Williamsburg, Va. 23187

COOPER-HEWITT MUSEUM. Smithsonian Institution, 2 East 91st Street, New York, N.Y. 10028

THE DECORATIVE ARTS TRUST. P.O. Box 1226, Camden, S.C. 29020

HISTORIC CHARLESTON FOUNDATION. 51 Meeting Street, Charleston, S.C. 29401

HISTORIC HOUSE ASSOCIATION OF AMERICA. 1600 H Street, N.W., Washington, D.C. 20006

HISTORIC SAVANNAH FOUNDATION. P.O. Box 1733, Savannah, Ga. 31402

METROPOLITAN MUSEUM OF ART. 82nd Street and Fifth Avenue, New York, N.Y. 10028

MUSÉE DES ARTS DÉCORATIFS. Palais du Louvre, Pavillon de Marsan, 107 rue de Rivoli, Paris, France 75000

MUSEUM OF ART, RHODE ISLAND SCHOOL OF DESIGN. 224 Benefit Street, Providence, R.I. 02903

MUSEUM OF EARLY SOUTHERN DECORATIVE ARTS. Drawer F, Salem Station, Winston-Salem, N.C. 27108

OLD ECONOMY VILLAGE. Harmonie Associates, Inc., 14th and Church Streets, Ambridge, Pa. 15003

OLD STURBRIDGE VILLAGE. Route 20, Sturbridge, Mass. 01566

NATIONAL PARK SERVICE. North Atlantic Regional Office, 15 State Street, Boston, Mass. 02109

DR. RONALD ROSSON HOUSE. 139 North 6th Street, Phoenix, Ariz. 85004

SOCIETY FOR THE PRESERVATION OF NEW ENGLAND ANTIQUITIES. 141 Cambridge Street, Boston, Mass. 02114

STOWE-DAY FOUNDATION. 77 Forest Street, Hartford, Conn. 06105

VICTORIA AND ALBERT MUSEUM. Exhibition and Cromwell Roads, London SW 1, England

THE VICTORIAN SOCIETY IN AMERICA. 219 East Sixth Street, Philadelphia, Pa. 19106

WINTERTHUR MUSEUM AND GARDENS. Route 52, Kennett Pike, Winterthur, Del. 19735

Wallpapers for Historic Buildings was edited by Gretchen Smith, associate editor, The Preservation Press. Christine Klimonda assisted in the production.

The book was designed by Robert Wiser and Marc Meadows, Marc Meadows and Associates, Washington, D.C. It was composed in Cloister Old Style by General Typographers, Inc., Washington, D.C., and printed by Wolk Press, Inc., Woodlawn, Md.

Most photographs of individual patterns were taken by J. David Bohl, staff photographer for the Society for the Preservation of New England Antiquities. In a few instances, photographs of patterns were supplied by the manufacturers.

ACKNOWLEDG-
MENTS